FROM NYMPH TO NUN IN NINE MONTHS

HOW TO SURVIVE RELATIONSHIPS

IAN VISSER

Bloomington, IN  Milton Keynes, UK

authorHOUSE®

AuthorHouse™
1663 Liberty Drive, Suite 200
Bloomington, IN 47403
www.authorhouse.com
Phone: 1-800-839-8640

AuthorHouse™ UK Ltd.
500 Avebury Boulevard
Central Milton Keynes, MK9 2BE
www.authorhouse.co.uk
Phone: 08001974150

First published by AuthorHouse   1/4/2007

ISBN: 978-1-4259-6177-0 (sc)

Printed in the United States of America
Bloomington, Indiana

This book is printed on acid-free paper.

TABLE OF CONTENTS

INTRODUCTION

'Nymph to nun' is primarily based on my personal experience from two marriages, the second still strong and healthy in most avenues. As I started sharing my "blessings" and frustrations with other friends I found that I was not the only male that had experienced similar encounters of 'the cold kind' from their spouse as priorities changed during their relationship. I've opted to share how the world of the women that I know changed from lover to mother over the 9 months, as well as draw from others experiences.

Most chapters have a '**Lesson to be learnt**' section; this is to give us insight as to what might be understood from the chapter, sort of a purpose or goal regarding the content and direction of the topic in hand.

Lesson to be learnt: *(An example of this insert, explaining the books motivation.)* This book as a whole is written for the purpose of understanding, not criticizing the other sex. Although the books title might seem a touch chauvinistic, I've tried to balance out opinions, views and findings from both sexes. Many of the contributors and those that have given sample chapters the "thumbs up" are women!

The book also has both a light funny (see cartoon on following page) and a more serious side. It also asks many questions, presents facts, answers some of the questions, and leaves a lot in the air intentionally for you to make your own decisions.

(Yep, if the above is you, there's a slight chance you might find more in common with many other males)

Now a good friend of mine has embarked on her interpretation of experiencing the male half, she's entitled it "from Hunk to Homer". Homer, as in the cartoon lad in the Simpson's – you remember, Bart's dad? The beer drinking, lazy, self-centered sloth whose character is often imposed on some husbands after marriage by the spouses, sometimes with reason?

As I believe that both men and women are also really quite okay and want the best for their partners too, we'll also be looking at circumstances that cause us to change once we've entered into the blessed union referred to as 'marriage'. These topics include religion, politics, careers, physical changes, responsibilities of child raising, and more.

Now some of my views and opinions might unintentionally offend, so I apologize before hand. Let me first explain my stance. Most of us search for a divine purpose to bless our existence on earth with a promise of a perfect afterlife.

As children we also entertain thoughts regarding the perfect marriage and feel that all the problems suffered by others will never affect us! This is arguably the main drive for many to search for both the perfect spouse and reason to exist. This is validated in the amount of marriages and religions in existence. Hence the decision to open my first comment regarding this topic:

1) I believe that ANY religion or belief that makes us as an individual a positive, kinder, more understanding, loving, and better person is a good thing and should be promoted. I have no intention of ridiculing or trying to sway any one from their belief. If you have any reservations that some of my questions and opinions might offend or lead you to stray, please refrain from reading further. The key to **successful** relationships begins with understanding and tolerating. When we can accept the others beliefs as a quest to become better and not necessarily a threat to us we would have conquered a HUGE obstacle in human relationships!

2) There are soooo many variations of beliefs with the opinion that they exclusively hold the divine truth, that toooo many could be wrong – I do not claim or even want to try and hint as to who might hold the answer for our divine purpose for walking this planet. Despite this, I would still like to encourage any positive studies that steer us away from killing our own species in the name of some delusional god or prophet. All I wish to accomplish is encourage us to keep an open mind and be prepared to share, learn and maybe even change as we experience various truths through our lives.

3) The phrase "**charity starts at home**" implies we look to ourselves first without blindly accepting any opinions or teaching as an

absolute. In other words we're all unique, so make sure whatever belief you embrace, that they, the leaders of the belief in question, answer ALL your questions. Any person who claims absolute authority with a view to condemn others is bound to lead to conflict, and an unhappy relationship at the least! Accepting certain "mysteries" is often the result of a leader, sect or religion not being able to answer what might be important to you! It might also be a warning light they aren't really interested in your individual curiosity as it distracts from their financial gain efforts, and/or time? I think that we might at least get closer the truth if we begin to try and understand ourselves. (With no guarantees of knowing if or when you might find it)

4) The average human, I'm tempted to say at least 95% of us are driven by good. Most people I encounter are really caring, want to help each other, do enjoy encouraging others, yep there are very few that are radical killers. And those that are that nasty can often arguably be declared insane? Or at the least there is medical proof of chemical imbalances in these deranged souls brains. Think about it, if say 25% of us were so deranged as to obliterate others not sharing their views, would you and I still be here?

So in short both sexes of the human race are really quite okay, so what the hell goes wrong and causes people that declare life long love and commitment to want to throttle the last breath out of each other after several (often short) years of trying to build what they set out to accomplish, the typical "Hollywood and they lived happily ever after theme"?

I also do realize that many do find this marital bliss, but sadly the statistics and successful divorces lawyers tend to lead me to believe they're in the minority. It also seems that many friends and acquaintances, although happy with their spouse, still yearn for more and do occasionally contemplate return to their single life, or for an affair. This I've found holds true for both sexes.

The purpose of this book:

To enlighten both sexes as to the others needs and frustrations. If just one relationship finds bliss from this book, then I'm happy. It made a difference to some-one…..

Before we read any further, we need to understand the two fictitious organs that are the theme for the book. These organs were created as a result of natural urges that lead us to mating and pairing eventually. These basic instinct drives are one of the most important underlying factors that often lead to success or failure in a relationship. Is you don't believe the importance of sex, please watch TV adverts and see all the "babes" and "hunks" that companies rely on to promote their items. The same can be said for movies.

Without sex none of us would be here, so we can debate that every person might have a strong subconscious drive to continue the human race, whether we're aware of it or not.

I challenge most of you to spend a few seconds thinking of your partner the first time you saw their certain "less visible" attributes while dating and that it did not arouse some or other primal feelings within you? (Perhaps they were in bathing clothes for example?)

The nymph and nun glands:

The **Nymph gland:**

This is a make believe entity, or rather organ that resides in the female brain influencing the sex drive of it's host. I took the first half of the word "nymphomaniac", a woman who really has to make love, get laid, enjoys sex, what ever you wish to call it. Most men hope to marry one, and often do before outside influences change and they find a few "alterations" in their life.

These outside influences are often stress related due to financial needs, children and us becoming parents, politics, religious convictions, physical changes as we age, and our own faulty human nature.

The **Nun gland:**

The equally fictitious organ that serves as its nymph counterpart, it's alter ego. I've taken this name from our Catholic counterparts, who have some in their faith that might fear sex as a great evil. I guess this goes to validate why some people might believe the human being is evil? Think about is, how can something good be created from an "evil" deed? Just kidding, but this religious belief likes us to accept that abstinence from sex often helps us focus on God. Mmm, so why is that we so often read of priests molesting alter boys? Haven't films and documentaries as well as tactless jokes been made on this unchallenged topic?

So in short, if the whole world adopted the nun glands stance we'd be the last generation of homosapien to walk the planet. In other words Gods purpose of "Go forth and multiply" would fall flat! Populations will dwindle until the last lad had better remember to turn off the lights and hand over the earth to the other animals.

I've also drawn to the conclusion that they, woman are not at fault, neither are men! I truly believe we have become victims of our social surrounding, with the likes of religious leaders, political leaders and the TV media not realizing the impact they have over the average human in society. Or maybe they do understand their role in society, and then exploit this for their own gain, so we now have, wait for it! (Fan fare of trumpets) "A conspiracy theory!"

I've also monitored friends who have had relationship "challenges" and how they dealt with and reacted to them. The idea was to see how and why people that start in these wonderful relationships change. Then retract into a mutual, not always peaceful, co existence. There could be out side factors that caused us humans to malfunction. If this is the case, then I'd really like to see if we could get rid of them.

The aim of this book is for men and woman to get some insight into each other, their needs and expectations of their partners. I'm hoping that my previously mentioned friend will write her similar book from her view as some might find the next few pages a bit chauvinistic or radical. I guess both species have a pre-conceived idea of how to see the other sex? – Just like the cartoon below that I received from a friend. (A woman I might add!)

Thanks to my friend – the potential woman writer. Once more my intention is not to criticize, but rather look at, study, laugh a bit, question and hopefully learn and build relationships. And if I fail to convey this intention please accept my sincerest apologies. I really believe that too many of the human species is just a little too inactive; this is why our political bullies get away with almost everything at the cost of our tax money and inconvenience.

Oh yeah, about the cartoons, these I ALL received from email, so I'm assuming that they're all public domain, so feel free to copy any of them. Any thing that makes you or some one else laugh, or at least smile should be shared?

I'm also concerned that some might find my religious beliefs offensive. I do believe in a creator, we may call him God if you like, but I think that man (and woman) often speak gross untruths about this person,

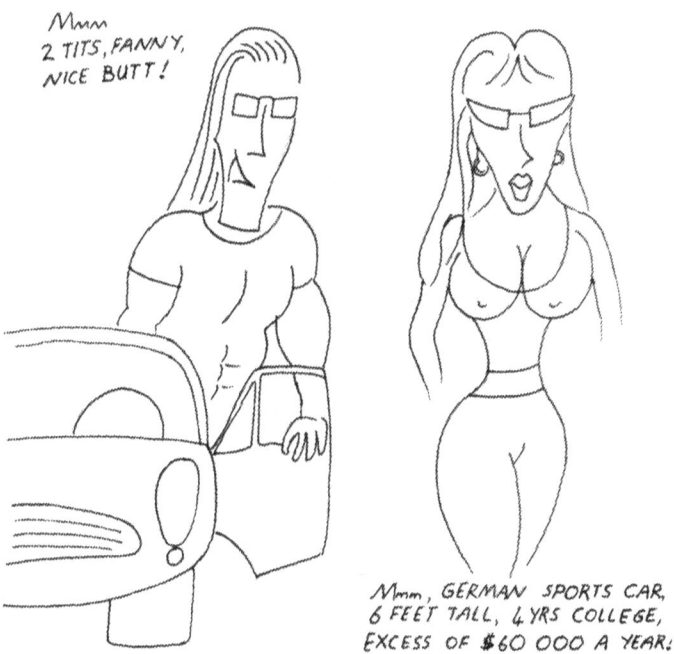

or maybe people? Or we tailor our spiritual creator(s) to our own needs and miss quote him/them to our advantage. Why is it so bad to accept that God might have peers, not servants? (Angels) Last question here "If mankind is made in Gods image, why is it incorrect to believe there is a Mr. and Mrs. God?"

Now it's important that you read the entire book before coming to any conclusions. This book was really both motivational and emotional to me while writing it. I've learnt so much about life as we know it that cannot be summed up in just one chapter, let alone a paragraph.

Although some sections might lean to certain way of thinking due to my own emotional response and understanding of certain topics, the conclusions in the later chapters suggest that "**Both boys and girls are generally pretty much okay – if they weren't, they wouldn't make the decision to team up in the first place.**" This quote you'll read again in later chapters.

The stories are all true, but the names and places have obviously been changed or left out to prevent lawyers from making even more money, and from 'tolerating' marriages from ending – hopefully once we understand each others needs better, failing marriages can be restored and enjoyed. There's no winner in divorce, just various levels of loss – especially for children!

Once more my hopes and wishes from these writings is that both species of the human race can get to live much happier together. I think we assume to often, I also think we quite unintentionally take each other for granted and simply expect our spouses to understand our stresses, accept our frustrations, and put up with our mood swings. (My wife has enlightened me that the word "**assume**" can be broken into three words, "**ass, u, me**", in other words assuming can make an "**Ass**" out of "**u**" and "**me**")

A friend summed this up perfectly when he said, "we often hurt the ones we love the most" – and this is a result of us assuming and expecting our partners to understand our unspoken thoughts. We so often expect a little too much from our mates, and they're just as humanly challenged as you are.

The more we can understand about ourselves the better control we can have of our own life, this in turn will free us from the restraints of society and media marketing tools that often try and mold us into believing that they know what we need best, often for their own financial gain? Who gave them the human manual?

I'm not expecting you to agree or accept my ideas and theologies, but to entertain them and apply the truths you've learnt through your walk of life to them where and when applicable. I believe you and I are both experiencing a living evolution. If we accept we've reached our point of no further growth and absolute knowledge we've become stagnant, and this is for me is both unacceptable and just really sad. Life is exciting and changes occur on many levels as we grow older and wiser.

I'd also encourage your wisdom to enlighten me regarding the thoughts and theories I have not been yet been exposed to, the more we share, the stronger and better the understanding of our existence will become.

My opinion on women? Well I wish more men were like them! They multitask better, wouldn't send their sons to kill each other, would care better for the children, and so much more. Okay, so now I've lost my male reading audience – please bear with me…

Let us grow…

Chapter 1: What A Wife Might Expect?

Let's open with a real sensitive issue. Yes, venturing to say what the female half of a marriage wants and needs are is quite a risky topic. Thinking on someone else's behalf has often led to conflict. The comments to follow are based on what women friends tell me as well as my personal two encounters exposed me to.

For me there is a distinct difference between a want and a need. For example, I want a sports car, perhaps a nice red BMW Z4 (even a 2nd hand one will do – any donors?), but in reality I need transport which an entrance level second hand 1400cc motorcar does really well.

Lesson to be learnt:
Try and imagine yourself loaded with the responsibilities you expect your spouse to handle. Live into their world and see if your expectations of them are still the same. Don't react too quickly and ask yourself, "What good will come out of my comments regarding my expectations of her"

I got this email from a friend; so let's introduce the lighter side of what a woman wants when searching for a husband.

The Husband Store!

A store that sells husbands has just opened in New York City, where a woman may go to choose a husband. Among the instructions at the entrance is a description of how the store operates. You may visit the store ONLY ONCE!

There are six floors and the attributes of the men increase as the shopper ascends the flights. There is, however, a catch, you may choose any man from a particular floor, or you may choose to go up a floor, but you cannot go back down except to exit the building! So, a woman goes to the Husband Store to find a husband.

*On the **first floor** the sign on the door reads:*
Floor 1 - These men have jobs and love the Lord.

*The **second floor** sign reads:*
Floor 2 - These men have jobs, love the Lord, and love kids.

*The **third floor** sign reads:*
Floor 3 - These men have jobs, love the Lord, love kids, and are extremely good looking. "Wow," she thinks, but feels compelled to keep going. She goes to the fourth floor and the sign reads:

***Floor 4** - These men have jobs, love the Lord, love kids, are drop- dead good looking and help with the housework."Oh, mercy me!" she exclaims, "I can hardly stand it!" Still, she goes to the fifth floor and the sign reads:*

***Floor 5** - These men have jobs, love the Lord, love kids, are drop- dead gorgeous, help with the housework, and have a strong romantic streak. She is so tempted to stay, but she goes to the sixth floor and the sign reads:*

***Floor 6** - You are visitor 74,363,012th to this floor. There are no men on this floor. This floor exists solely as proof that women are impossible to please!*

Thank you for shopping at the Husband Store. Watch your step as you exit the building, and have a nice day!

You won't believe how many men will, or rather have appreciated this joke, maybe even related to it on one level or another. So let's have a quick giggle on the men's weakness from a woman's perspective. Yes, girls don't always think that highly of us superior males either. (Just kidding folks) And below we have another view of how the fairer sex sees us – not overly flattering?

Men are like....

1. Men are like – Laxatives. They irritate the shit out of you.

2. Men are like – Bananas. The older they get, the less firm they are.

3. Men are like - Weather. Nothing can be done to change them.

*4. Men are like – Blenders. You need One,
   but you're not quite sure why.*

*5. Men are like - Chocolate Bars. Sweet, smooth,
   & they usually head right for your hips.*

6. Men are like - Commercials. You can't believe a word they say.

7. Men are like - Department Stores. Their clothes are always 1/2 off.

*8. Men are like - Government Bonds. They
   take sooooooooo long to mature.*

9. Men are like – Mascara. They usually run at the first sign of emotion.

10. Men are like -Popcorn. They satisfy you, but only for a little while.

*11. Men are like - Snowstorms. You never know when they're
   coming, how many inches you'll get or how long it will last.*

12. Men are like - Lava Lamps. Fun to look at, but not very bright!

*13. Men are like - Parking Spots. All the good ones
   are taken, the rest are handicapped.*

So we're off to a great beginning, it seems that on flippant level men and women don't think that highly of each other! Yet we spend our entire life trying to pair up with one! It must be our internal programming – we'll chat about this later.

I'm still nervous on this topic and wondering if typing any further on this topic is a great idea. I'd hate to have either sex think I'm stereo typing! But I must admit there are lots of common situations found in relationships. On speaking with married male friends for example, I found that when I admitted my sex life had ground to an anal, I mean annual event I found many 'previous sexually active' men admitted similar problems during marriage.

The drive to go from lover to mother:
I dare say that many women at some point in their life find their biological clock stressing an urgency to test out their womb. To make sure that this organ functions correctly means they need the assistance of the male's lower brain. Perhaps many males are prepared to share simply for the pleasure while entertaining the fear for pregnancy? Many married males friends shared that once their wife has become a mother their whole priority schedule changed.

Well this is not really surprising. Women have the awesome privilege of being able to give birth, they actually feel the growth from fetus to first born, I wonder how we males would react if we shared the same experience? My tummy growth is due to beer and lack of exercise!

Well after the nine months, our spouse goes through labor, and judging by my first hand experience of watching, it is more than painful! Bear in mind that this is their climax after morning sickness, nausea, lack of sleep, sore back in some cases, careful diet and health changes, fear of miscarriage, hormonal swings, and discomfort of a large body in many cases. So the immediate rewards for continuing the human race are not pleasant.

During this time we males only have one problem, to live with them and understand their needs. Our load is really light when compared to their physical and emotional guys, bear in mind we planted that seed, so it's not too much to ask to try and tolerate their mood swings, and other problems.

Now to the women who during pregnancy feel their size is unattractive! Please do not generalize all males, many of us are in awe of your strength to go through this, and find you even more beautiful. Similarly, if you find your changes are making you act completely out of character with a negative impact, please get a doctor to help. Although us boys cannot experience your evolutionary process, anything that can make the trip more pleasant should be pursued.

Many of the newly developed traits continue from pregnancy to child raising, so both partners need to build on every positive opportunity they can. The only down side from my half is that my responsibility only starts nine months later than my wife's. Now if only the males hormonal drive had an easier to control on-off switch?

Comments like such as the following listed were often heard from my male friends:

1: Their wives often say, "All you think of is sex!"

2: Another favorite female quote is: "I'm tired from the day and have a headache." To validate this one, the media even made fun of this recurring situation by running an advert about headache tablets to avoid the wife's pains.

3: I'm sure many men have heard "It's that time of the month." Now I actually have heard some women say that sex during a period is better as senses are more pleasurable. It does sound as if there's hope for the fairer sex thanks to the few who seem to still enjoy it. Pity that most seem to be single or not yet graduated to parent.

4: I want to watch TV. This is great, it's very reassuring to ANY spouse that they take a solid 2nd place to a flickering tube with cheap sound! Certainly makes me feel good about myself on many occasions – not!

5: Then there a few woman who because they don't find themselves attractive, think their spouses don't either. Okay so there are a few jerk men out there that expect their wives to like super models, but not all of us are that shallow. My wife is 41, and in my eyes she's attractive, super sexy, just stunning. The downer is that she thinks I'm just being nice – this is real sad!

6: And for those with children, has your wife ever said: "What if little Johnny or Jenny catches us?" This one is the lamest excuses. I'm sure that you've experienced your parents shouting at each other one time or another and this was almost okay? I dare say that they didn't try to hide that they were pissed off with each other. But should you catch them loving each other? The hugest of sins!

With point 6 I'm not suggesting we intentionally make love in front of our children, but I'd rather be stumbled upon enjoying and loving my relationship with my partner than screaming at her. Discretion as to where to have sex is obvious, but perhaps if children were more open to this there might be less of a fascination to this great taboo, and arguably less teen pregnancies, terminations, etc?

One thought I have is that once our subconscious purpose to pair up has been fulfilled, the primary drive is satisfied, unless the need for more children is present. This means we might find ourselves in a situation that we never anticipated, which could lead to many disappointments. Thankfully there are relationships that do succeed; we need to learn from these people, preferably before we engage in lifelong commitment!

I believe that both sex education and family education need to be a compulsory subjects at ALL schools, with more focus on the latter. This I believe in turn might reduce divorces, STDS, and even the need for AID's education in the future. The result? Happier families!

So what goes wrong?
It's so ironic that war, along with all the its gross pictures are displayed as movies, books, the TV news, TOYS (so we train our kids the joy of killing at just post toddler! Go check out the toyshops.) While two consenting adults are banned you can freely purchase soldiers, guns, killing machines and monsters. No wonder society is so screwed. Yep, it's also okay to have hostile images of men killing and shooting the crap out of each other in the name of freedom. While freedom of loving your partner is restrained. Not all porn is bad people; I do not condone animal sex, group sex, or children sex. (That's just sick!). You yourself are the living breathing result of two consenting adults having sex and I hope the 'deed' was rather beautiful!

Now what does a wife want?

My guess is as follows, not that I achieve this as often as I'd like to due to my own selfish needs, imperfect sense of logic and fairness, but I do try. Well I think woman like and expect the following:

1: To be loved.

2: To be respected.

3: To be treated as equal.

4: To be encouraged.

(Sort of sounds like wedding vows so far?)

5: To share family responsibilities such as housework, making food on occasion, maybe doing laundry? Cleaning the car, looking after garden, waking up at 3 in the morning if junior is ill.

6: For those where husband is the only breadwinner – some sort of financial allowance or rather independence. This topic can be sensitive.

7: To have their biological needs respected and understood with lot of love, caring and patience.

There are other expectations that I think we both have in common. We both need a certain amount of space and togetherness. The trouble is when the two opposite needs arrive at the same time! She wants company and I need space, or the reverse. Understanding is every bit as important as fulfilling your needs.

Financial needs are often relationship killers too. Especially when the one partner feels their efforts are unappreciated, or they believe the other is side stepping their responsibility. The solution here? Talk about what you need, discuss solutions – two brains are better than one? Formulate a plan to work towards a mutual success or goal. Even consider external help, a councilor of sorts, should you have conflicting opinions. Remember that although your thoughts might not agree, you BOTH want the same end result!

A level of independence is crucial. After 12 years of school, being a child, perhaps a form of post school studies, we're now big boys and girls called "adults". So the last thing anyone needs is to be treated like a kid and having to need to report to ones spouse on everything when your 20+ years of age, even more so when you're 30, 40 or 50yrs in existence!

For example women might entertain a need for cosmetic appearances – often for us boys! Similarly men might prioritize work for financial gain – for the girls. See? We're both actually often trying to make the other happy, but perhaps come across selfish when doing so! Perhaps "space" and "independence" are very closely linked, it's how we let our partners entertain these needs that are crucial!

For a quick overview of what both sexes want of all ages, I asked some acquaintances to list 10 things that they would like from an IDEAL relationship. Chapter 4 lists some of the answers, they are quite interesting.

Chapter 2: What A Man Might Expect?

Lesson to be learnt:
Okay guys, this is on your behalf, for those who don't agree, I apologise. There seems to be a misconception that many non-gay men often hide emotions, but also would love to cry but fear this as a sign of weakness. What I'm trying to say to you girls is that it's not easy being a man either. We also need you to think before you act, to live yourselves into the male world – hey, living with a woman is not that easy either, so give us a break. But on the overall the same message is carried through from the first chapter.

Let's start with a light-hearted look at how some men see their feminine half. The sad truth is that although the letter was a joke email from a friend, yes a woman, there are of us "willy carriers" that are actual idiots and lend some sort of truth to John's story below as he tries to 'stand up' for his wife. Let's laugh…

A LETTER FROM JOHN TO THE EDITOR

Dear Sir,

Please be aware that as your wives age, it is harder for them to maintain the same quality of housekeeping as when they were younger. When you notice this, try not to yell at them. Some are oversensitive, and there is nothing worse than an oversensitive woman.

My name is, John. Let me relate how I handled the situation with my wife, Martha. When I was laid off from my consulting job and took early retirement in April, it became necessary for Martha to get a full-time job, both for extra income and for the health insurance benefits we needed.

Shortly after she started working, I noticed she was beginning to show her age. I usually get home from the golf course about the same time she gets home from work, and although she knows how hungry I am, she rests an hour or so before she starts dinner. I don't yell at her. Instead, I tell her to take her time and just wake me when she gets dinner on the table. I generally have lunch in the Men's Grill at the club, so eating out is not reasonable. I'm ready for some home-cooked grub when I hit that door. She used to do the dishes as soon as we finished eating. But now, it's not unusual for them to sit on the table for several hours after dinner. I do what I can by diplomatically reminding her several times each evening that they won't clean themselves. I know she appreciates this, as it does seem to motivate her to get them done before she goes to bed. I really think my old business as a consultant helps a lot. Telling people what they ought to do is one of my strong points.

Also, now that she has gotten older, she does seem to get tired so much more quickly. Our washer and dryer are in the basement, and sometimes she says she just can't make another trip down those steps. I don't make a big issue of this, just as long as she finishes up the laundry the next evening. I'm willing to overlook her shortcomings in this area. Unless I need something ironed to wear to the Monday lodge meeting, or to the Wednesday and Saturday poker club, or to Tuesday and Thursday's bowling, I'll tell her to wait until the next evening to do the ironing. This gives her a little more time to do some of those odds and ends like shampooing the dog, vacuuming or dusting. If I had a really bad day on the course and it was wet and muddy, and my clubs are a mess, I let her clean them, you know, getting the grit off the grips and a little light Brillo on the club faces.

Since my golf bag is heavy, I lift it out of the trunk for her. Women are delicate, have weak wrists and can't lift heavy stuff as good as men. But I had to tell her that I don't like to be wakened during my after-golf nap, so rather than bother me, she can put them back in the trunk when she's finished.

Another symptom of aging is complaining. For example, she will say that it is difficult for her to find time to pay the monthly bills during her lunch hour. But boys, we take 'em for better or worse, so I just smile and offer encouragement. I tell her to stretch it out over two or even three days. That way she won't have to rush so much. I also remind her that missing lunch completely now and then wouldn't hurt her any (if you know what I mean). I like to think tact is one of my strong points.

When doing simple jobs, she seems to think she needs more rest periods. She had to take a break when she was only half finished mowing the yard. I try not to make a scene. I'm a fair man. I tell her to fix herself a nice, big, cold glass of fresh squeezed lemonade and just sit for a while. And, as long as she is making one for herself, she may as well make one for me too, then take her break by my hammock. That way we can talk until I fall asleep. I know that I probably look like a saint in the way I support Martha, but I'm not saying that showing this much consideration is easy.

Many men will find it difficult. Some will find it impossible! Nobody knows better than I do, how frustrating women get as they get older. However, guys, even if you just use a little more tact and less criticism of your aging wife because of this letter, I will consider that writing it was well worthwhile.

After all, we are put on this earth to help each other

Regards,
John

EDITOR'S NOTE:
**John died suddenly Thursday, May 19th. He was found with a Calloway extra long 50-inch Big Bertha Golf Driver rammed up his rectum with only two inches of grip showing. His wife Martha

*was arrested, but after the jury read this letter, they accepted her defence that he accidentally sat on it. She was released from custody on Friday. – **Now, back to the book..***

Let's return back to our theme, "nymph to nun". When some of us boys act like John here, it's no wonder why the nun glad throttles the life out of the nymph gland. But luckily, like the women, there are quite a few really great specimens of the more understanding male sex. The sad part is that quite often opposites attract and the nice pair with the 'not-so-nice'. Could this be what fuels the bitterness that is often found within many marriages?

As for I would like from my wife:

1: To be loved.

2: To be respected.

3: To be treated as equal.

4: To be encouraged.

(Sort of sounds like wedding vows, from the past chapter?)

5: For her to realize that she gave us the most
   wonderful gift, our little boy.

6: For those where we share the income, that we both enjoy some
   rewards for our work, provided all our needs are taken care of
   first. This topic can be sensitive, especially if one partner feels
   they're carrying the family while the other is not trying as hard.

7: To realize that when I want to make love to her that it's
   not just a screw or casual intercourse, and that I would
   love to touch and spoil her physically and emotionally.

There are many needs that both men and women have, these get discussed in later chapters, but to let you know where I'm going with the book, here are some needs I think everyone needs:

Love, understanding, caring, listening, time alone, time together, sex, feeling of belonging, success, challenges, rest, reassurance, and more..

Yes, I really miss the active sex life we used to share, and I sincerely do wish I could shut this drive of mine down to avoid unnecessarily conflict and feelings of guilt for having them. This is another common finding I've learnt from many other married men.

Even though I do feel that women experience a radical change during the 9month crossover, it is not an excuse or license to unfairly bully us with the concept, "I had it worse than you". I dare say this plot has also been played out in many relationships, with a counter productive result?

Personally I think that as we evolve from partners to parents we need to realize we are now big boys and girls. We need to try and understand each other a bit more. An increase of tolerance, patience, and living into each other's needs could have a positive affect as we can appreciate the drive of our biological needs.

Again, I think our schooling systems could consider a stronger focus on this form of education. The rewards that come from a happy family are endless. I thank my present wife for her love, patience and understanding.

And as for the fights? I'm sure we'll have a few more as we turn gray, but with her willingness to help work the problems through I'm optimistic. We both mess up when tired, or when we don't have all the facts correct, the human design is flawed I guess.

The lesson to be learnt here?
Don't rush marriage or children. These can be the greatest blessings you'll ever experience or a catastrophe. May you never experience the latter.

Chapter 3: Friends Stories

Lesson to be learnt.
To understand first hand what others think about life, marriage and relationships. In other words an outside view, not just my opinions.

I thought it might be interesting to print some stories from friends that I asked to write about their opinions, expectations and experiences in life. You'll notice they're all quite nice people, well I think they're actually fantastic and I wish I could thank them personally by name in this book, but we decided not to.

I have not altered any grammar, or changed words, added sentences or omitted anything. Except a spell check courtesy of my PC's software.

Story 1: A woman's story
(This is from a woman, married, no children, 24yrs old, works as does her husband. First marriage, and may it stay that way. They're both awesome people)

Here are her writings:
At the "tender" age of 24 I have had my fair share of heartache and disappointments. Although my life experiences might seem limited considering my age, I consider myself to be much more mature than my peers.

While some of my friends still live with their parents, I have had to fend for myself at the age of 18. They moved to the Freestate when I was still in standard 9, and I had to live with my grandmother. It was my decision to stay as I did not want to move just before my final year in a school I have been attending since standard 6 and for the first time in my life I was chosen as a prefect in my matrix year and I didn't want to throw that away.

Living with my grandmother was torture to say the least. On the day I wrote my final exam my sister came to fetch me and I left for Paarl. While my friends were fortunate enough to study at University (my life dream), I had patrons staring at my boobs (when I still had them) having to wait at tables to earn a living. Although I hold a lot of animosity towards my parents for not being able to give me the opportunity in life that I believe everyone deserves, being in the "real" world much earlier than my peers have made me a stronger person. Maybe better planning in their lives would have changed ours?

Life has taught me some of its ugly lessons. I must say some days I think to myself that I never imagined it to be so crappy when I was still a teenager. For most of my childhood years since the age of about 8 I can remember growing up being poor. So I've always had this utopia in my head that I will do everything right and not end up like my parents. So far it's going great, but life isn't all I imagined it would be. I know I might sound like Dr. Doom, but don't get me wrong, in spite of a lot of things I am happy.

Since I can remember I have been saying that I don't want to lead a meaningless existence that I want to be remembered as someone who contributed something wonderful to society and life as a whole. I have yet to get to that point, if ever...

There must be more to life than what we know and have now? For instance, I don't believe that we could be the only planet with life on it? There must be other planets and galaxy's where some form of life exists? Why are we so special to have the sun all for ourselves? I don't know why I am here; all I can say is that life is almost never fair. The more money and power you have, the more you get. If you are poor, you're more than likely to stay poor (although there are exceptions). Us Christians like to believe that "Everything happens for a reason", ever heard that line?? I seldom if ever see a reason in some things, especially when you turn on the telly and yet another 6-month-old baby has been raped!! So where's the reason in that???

So what about talking about something good for a change? I'm a pretty open-minded person and there are a lot of good in the world to that I like to believe in. The most important one of all for me is love. There is possibly no better motivational feeling (except for hate, the opposite, ironic?).

I believe that you can really love someone with your every being. I believe in true love and everlasting love, but is there such thing as a perfect relationship? My answer is plain and simple, NO! How can a perfect relationship exist between two imperfect creatures? Everyone has flaws and NO ONE is perfect.

My philosophy is that there is no such thing as a perfect relationship, but to love an imperfect person perfectly. It's not easy, especially when your partner is totally different than you. Like in my case. My husband is a rugby dop & chop kind of guy as apposed to me, the emotional thinker who loves classical music and writing poetry! (for the non-Afrikaans – dop means drink, as in beer or wine, etc.)

It's funny, I always imagined my perfect partner behind a black Baby Grand singing me a love song, but instead I married a caveman! I guess it's true what they say about opposites attract? So you see life isn't all-bad. I'm blessed with a loving faithful husband, a blessed marriage and friends and family I would die for. Sure every marriage has it's up's and downs but for the most part I couldn't have asked for a better partner. I think the key is to be open to your partner. They won't know what your needs are if you keep it to yourself.

It's hard to be honest to someone you love if it's something they might not want to hear but what's the alternative? My husband was my first in everything. I might not have had more than one partner in life, but I do believe you can be with only one person your whole life and still know what true love is. I'm thankful to have found my life partner at a very young age. Relationships are very hard work and I think people forget that sometimes. People get married and expect everything to stay the same. So they go their separate ways living day in and day out and never once think of working on their relationship. It could be the smallest thing, sending an "I love you" sms out of the blue, picking a rose from your garden and placing it on your partner's pillow. Or after a long days work running a bath with candles and letting your partner have some "me" time. Nothing extravagant and it doesn't cost a cent.

So why don't most people do this? They stopped working on it and believe the relationship will automatically stay the same and it doesn't. So bottom line: If you truly love someone and you want to make it work, you have to do some hard work to maintain that relationship. There is no such thing as the "perfect relationship" we so often see in a romantic movie, and we have to get that idea out of our heads. But the key is to live in such a way that you strive towards a relationship that's as good as it gets.

Bottom line: Life is what you make of it. Maybe we should start to enjoy life more every day instead of wondering too much of things that we have no answer or control over. Life is shorter than we think. I heard this one saying that struck a chord: "God give me the serenity to accept the things I can't change, to change the things I can and the wisdom to tell the difference."

Story ends here.
Story number 2: another woman's tale
(The next story is from a single divorced woman, age 50, two children, and works.)

Here are her writings:
Some people lay claim to "love at first sight" with their partners and accept and love them for who and what they are. Otherwise, it's a case of initial attraction like looks, personality etc, as they are, when they meet. Some never understand that what you see is what you get.

Lots of spadework is done to attract the other in those first wondrous meetings and then it gets down to the nitty gritty of, especially women, trying to change their man. (Why would they want to do that when what and who they met is what and who they fell in love with initially?)

For a lucky few, there is some adjustment, some compromise as their relationship moves to serious, moving in and/or marriage. There is a settling-in (or down) period with some compromise to normal things, quite acceptable to both - their love for each other a huge plus at this time.

I can never understand, when one feels that one has met their love/life partner, why one would want to change them. Surely they wouldn't be good enough initially. Women are always guilty of trying to change their man ie less drinking, no more men friends, live sport with the guys now out of the question - "you don't have any time for me" gets thrown in, less drinking, more help in the house, and the list goes on and on.

Well this is when the bitching starts - and suddenly the poor husbands have to attend dinner parties (wife's friends only - who could stand to include the chisel-edged rugged bugger in casuals in this set up!?) More trips to the grocery store - a really shitty chore for some, gardening becomes a chore when getting shouted at to do it.

Men too, but on a much smaller ratio, can also be guilty of trying to change their woman - in a colleague's case, her man dictated the clothes she had to wear ie long skirts, only blue gray & black in color, no make up, hideously long hair tied up in a bun every day, to make her unattractive to other men.

And in my case, more make up of his choice, his choice of clothes and shoes, diet clinic (weighing only 64kg's - so fat huh) His favorite words "stop embarrassing me". A hectic Hitler dictator type. Unsightly in his eyes at 6 months pregnant on and when miracle child born, too ugly to keep, must give up for adoption! And then wonders why, after 2 years, finds his bags packed at the front door. "What did I do wrong?"

End of story two. An arguably unusually bias towards the boys favor? But still food for thought!

Story number 3: At least the woman have lots to say in this chapter!
(This friend is 52, divorced, no children. I left all the words in uppercase, as she has typed them, as these comments are obviously important to her. It's interesting to see opinions regarding marriages!)

Here are her writings:
At this stage of my life, all I am interested in is having peace and harmony, LOTS OF FUN while I still can - if someone, with the same interests as I have, comes along, well who knows. I am NOT ANTI-MEN. I find them more interesting to talk to than women.

Not convinced that marriage is the way to go if you do not intend having children. But that's my opinion. Think I've been on my own too long now. Become very selfish in a way. DON'T WANT COMMITMENTS OR OBLIGATIONS. LOVE TO COME AND GO AS I PLEASE. NO ONE TO TELL ME WHAT TO DO AND WHEN AND HOW.

I had an abusive marriage. Took forever to get out of it. I knew after the first 3 months it was a mistake. But being as stupid as I am, always thought it would get better HA HA HA. Anyway, after 16 and a half years of feeling absolutely "dead" inside, I am now HAPPILY DIVORCED going on 10 and a half years. Advice for females (or males) LISTEN TO YOUR PARENTS WHEN THEY TELL YOU "THAT PERSON IS NOT GOOD FOR YOU". They know what they are talking about. They can see what u can't. (love is blind!!!)

End of story three.
Please notice the need to be her own boss, this is so important! Try dictating to your partner and there's a risk of mutiny in later years. Remember, the only thing we cannot buy is our time lost. **Be very careful how you invest your life!**

It's really great to have such great buddies that are prepared to share life experiences so openly! This info you normally pay a fortune for via a biography of same famous person. You seldom get to read true stories from the average person.

Another interesting comment here, in favor of the fairer sex, is that I mailed an equal amount of men and woman alike regarding their life experience opinions. Only woman have replied so far! In the defense of my breasted counterparts I find that on average, do women get the job done quicker and more effectively?

Come on boys, you're letting my team down. The requests for this chapter were typed on the 23rd May, so let's see towards the end of the book what further responses I've had.

What I'd like us to observe is that many of the opinions regarding life, relationships, and our own drive for purpose is for the good. If only good people were more assertive is a possible argument, or at least as assertive as the bully. The catch is one comment I heard which went something like this. "Be careful to argue with bullies, or unreasonable people as you lower your standards to theirs."

Well with this in mind could some one PLEASE explain why we must tolerate their shit? Secondly, by letting the bullies have their way, EVERY ONE suffers! Even the bully as he might be under the illusion that he's actually trying to help by enforcing his will for "the greater picture" – so what now? My conclusion is that a bully thought of this clever phrase to let less assertive or nervous people feel good about their silent non-challenge.

Story 4: A man's story
(This lad is married, 4 children, 41yrs old, and works, as does his wife. First marriage, and may it stay that way. He has less conventional approach regarding religion and is extremely well educated as well as a successful programmer for an international company.)

Here are his writings:
It is in human nature to believe in the supernatural, in all forms and guises. Once humans realise that they must rely on themselves to get ahead, teach their children to trust in their parents and believe in them as their own personal gods, and love one another without threat of evil, miracles will happen.

Worship the truth that lies in the world around them; the evolution of the creatures and the beauty of nature.

Be thankful to others who are actually the church, the real people who as a community help each other.

Till the children themselves become accountable for their lives, and can stand up and become gods themselves, not in the name of some 'supernatural being, but in the name of reality and truth, then the world will be at peace and the human race will start evolving again!

* Don't sit back and hope that an entity will save
  you; you have the power to save yourself!

* Don't convince those that life starts after
  death, for then life means nothing,

* Don't lie and pretend, be honest, accountable and proud of the
  decisions you make, for they have come from your own being,

* Trust in yourself to make the right decisions for yourself
  and those who you are accountable to, to those who
  look up to you, for your action have repercussions which
  will expand over a wide range for a long time.

* Evil only exists in the human, created by him, perpetuated by
  him and practised widely by him. It has no other meaning; the
  human has not evolved enough to move beyond this behaviour.
  Look to the animals, who exist without blame, then look back
  at the human who blames the supernatural influence for its
  mistakes and relies in another supernatural being to forgive
  its mistakes. Don't make the mistakes, be accountable?

* Allow all to follow their own path, whatever it may be! Be gracious
  and kind, never judge, for all end up the in the same way.

Ever mind the rule of three
An' it harm none, do as ye will'

Story 5: A man's story

(This lad is married, 2 children, 33yrs old, and has AIDS, he has a possible 6months to two years left I'm told. It's his second marriage, and they're extremely happy despite his predestined early departure from us. The email received back was not quite what I expected, but I think there's a valuable lesson as to how we place our priorities. His own priorities are quite different from ours I do to different time line he finds himself in.)

Here are his writings:

Normal life is getting dressed in clothes that you buy on credit for work, driving trough traffic in a car that you are still paying for, in order to get to a job that you need so badly so you can pay for the clothes, car and the house that you leave empty all day in order to afford to live in it.

Time line comments:

Well these comments came in as from the 25 June onwards

Chapter 4: What Others Expect

Lesson to be learnt.
To find out what others actually do expect from their spouses. These are not my writings, although I might agree with most of the comments I'll leave it to your discretion to decide which comments I don't. I initially asked for stories, this is what led to chapter 3, but after a really slow response on life experiences I decided to ask others for summaries in point form of their expectations from the other sex. Now the males began to reply!

Human spec list 1:
From 22ry old, woman, single, no children, working and independent.

Ok...Things that woman expect from men which would influence the relationships survival,

Its all the things they don't think of!! Not because they don't care but because they just can't. Its so difficult to say because men (make us believe that they) need to be reminded about EVERYTHING!

These are a few things that I expect - and in my mind - these are the things
I expect him to do/say that will assure me he still cares/loves me.

1) Always give me a kiss hello/goodbye

2) Ask how my day was (even if you don't actually care)

3) Talk to me (not "aha" "ya" "mm" etc)

4) Fill me in on your whereabouts as they change

4) Consider me as my own person with my own responsibilities

5) Tell me I look beautiful when you can
   see I've made a special effort

6) Comment on new clothes (if it's bad - "oh
   that's new!" & a kiss will do)

7) I expect at least one call during the course of my working day
   just so I know he's thinking of me (I wait for this everyday)

8) I do expect help at home such as picking up after
   yourself (dirty clothes in basket, dishes in sink, etc.

9) I expect him to make an effort on my birthday or
   our anniversary to do something special

10) I expect him to accompany me to functions and parties
    we have been invited to as a couple regardless of whether
    he wants to be there or not (at least to make an appearance
    unless he has previous arrangements - compromise)

11) I expect him to allow me my opinion (agree to disagree) and
    be patient with me when my (acknowledged) flaws surface.

1) I don't expect him to understand me - only TRY

2) I don't expect him to love me - but if he does
   (and he should) TRY and show me

3) I wouldn't expect him to financially support me - just contribute.

AND..... I DEMAND mind blowing sex every night!

Ha ha! That's all! Too much to ask??...............I think not! Hehehe!

Human spec list 2:
From 38ry old, man, married, one child. Oh yeah, he's a musician too.

1. A lot of sex

2. Keep the fridge stocked with beer

3. Sewing

4. Blowjobs

5. More beer

6. Cooking

7. Cleaning and a bit of ironing for days with real shirts in them

8. Better keep fit and look good all the time

9. Don't hide the remote control, other useful items or man toys

10. Threesomes with lesbians

Bonus: 11. Wash the car occasionally..

And anyone who says anything else is just not being honest...

Hey, he's also the first male to reply, and within 2 days of my email requests – thanks lad. I also know him quite well, so I'm not sure if all his comments are completely honest?

Human spec list 3:
From a psychologist, married, no children. I was keen to se what the professionals thought about relationships and my own psychologist was kind enough to let me have these thoughts. I believe these comments to be the best and most accurate expectations from any partner. Although it's a lot more serious than the person number2, it sort of sums up number 1 quite well.

1: Compassion

2: Endurance.

3: Coexistence.

4: Enjoys life

5: Intelligence

6: A sense of humor

7: Loves nature.

8: An ability to share emotions

9: Direct communication

What I found to be quite strange was the lack of response from all those I mailed regarding what they would like from their spouse. It is now 1 August, 2006, and no further replies.

CHAPTER 5: TO GENERALIZE, OR NOT TO GENERALIZE

As humans, we try and stereo type others, whether intentional or not. This is some sort of built in parameter requirement that we use to shortcut the time spent to get to know the actual person. Although this instinct is often correct and has saved us endless hours when it comes to pursuing a doomed relationship or a business deal, we also tend to some times loose the opportunity to get to know others, their true motives, and in turn this might cause relationships to fail, nymph glands to malfunction, unnecessary confrontations, and more.

Although this concept does lead to some racial, religious and relationship preconceived theories such as "blonds are dumb, men think with their penis, politicians lie, blacks are inferior", and sooo much more. Check this mail on the women and their nationalities vs their sex motivations.

"DATING RITUALS"

ENGLISH WOMEN
First date:	You get to kiss her goodnight.
Second date:	You get to grope all over and make out.
Third date:	You get to have sex, but only in the missionary position.

IRISH WOMEN
First Date:	You both get blind drunk and have sex.
Second Date:	You both get blind drunk and have sex.
20th Anniversary:	You both get blind drunk and have sex.

ITALIAN WOMEN

First Date: You take her to a play and an expensive restaurant.

Second Date: You meet her parents and her Mom makes spaghetti and meatballs.

Third Date: You have sex, she wants to marry you and insists on a 3-carat ring.

5th Anniversary: You already have 5 kids together and hate the thought of having sex.

6th Anniversary: You find yourself a girlfriend.

JEWISH WOMEN

First Date: You get dynamite head.

Second Date: You get more great head.

Third Date: You tell her you'll marry her and never get head again.

CHINESE WOMEN

First date: You get to buy her an expensive dinner, but nothing happens.

Second date: You buy her an even more expensive dinner. Nothing happens again.

Third date: You don't even get to the third date and you already realized nothing is going to happen.

INDIAN WOMEN

First date: Meet her parents.

Second date: Set the date of the wedding.

Third date: Wedding night.

AFRICAN AMERICAN WOMEN

First Date: You get to buy her a real expensive dinner.

Second Date: You get to buy her and her girlfriends a real expensive dinner.

Third Date: You get to pay her rent.

Tenth Date: She's pregnant by someone other than you.

MEXICAN WOMEN

First Date:	You buy her an expensive dinner, get drunk on Tequila, and have sex in the back of her car.
Second Date:	She's pregnant.
Third Date:	She moves in. One week later ~ her mother, father, his girlfriend, her two sisters, her brother, all of their kids, her grandma, her father's girlfriend's mother, her two cousins, her sister's boyfriend and his three kids move in and you live on rice and beans for the rest of your life in your home that used to be nice, but now looks like a home along the Rio Grande.

The point
Don't you just love Irish woman?

Now before you think that I'm the guilty one for this list of unflattering rather dubious opinions, please remember that some one sent this to me, and that it made many laugh, yep, I'm guilty of the giggles too!

Well back to my book. I'm very tempted to say that every person walking the 3rd rock from the sun has at some time or other assumed some one else's intentions and been wrong! I'm also not suggesting that the assumption in question was intentional, or done out of spite. It was probably as a result of our faulty programming and design – being human has it down side?

Now imagine this, a possible marriage co-existence scenario. Both the sexes of the marriage have been subjected to opinions regarding the attitude and responsibilities of the husband and wife; this could have arguably subliminally conditioned us regarding our interpretation of our spouses' intentions?

I've listed a few preconceived comments on how some might view their spouse. Before you say, 'nah, that's not me', think about all the cartoons, jokes, emails and tv-shows that have shared a similar approach!

What some woman assume about men:

1: Sit in front of TV drinking beer/ wine/ what ever.
2: Never help around at home.
3: Like to have affairs is a general requirement for many husbands.
4: Just want sex from their wives.
5: Have little or NO personal hygiene habits.
6: Would rather be at the pub than at home with family.

What men think about women:

1: Always sit on the phone to friends.
2: Spend infinite time with manicures,
   pedicures, cosmetically shallow.
3: Spend all day wanting to shop and spend husband's money.
4: Use sex to snare a husband, after marriage
   and family, sex often stops.
5: Overkill on personal hygiene habits.
6: Would rather watch soapies and reality TV
   than spend time with family.

Well the above has been themes for many humor, arguments, and even divorce! Please don't forget the basic plot to any soapy, as well as other movies?

So we have this subconscious preconception of our spouse, that some really even do live up to! So is it any real surprise that our fairer sex goes from Nymph to Nun in nine months? (I really hope my friend has got "typists finger" already or on her 3rd pen, from writing her book to be called "From Hunk to Homer ".)

As this is still the beginning of my wild ramblings on the married species, I'd like to point out that the married person is really a completely different species to the single human! We can almost compare marriage to form of human evolution, but instead of taking a few million years, we change or are subjected to a changing partner in months!

Memory plays a cruel joke on both sexes, it reminds us of how our lives were before we paired up and 'mated'. This often makes the married, now family responsible, yearn for the 'good old days'. Discipline is the key word here, emotions mess with logic and gets quite confusing, so we need to help and understand our partners needs.

For those that are still single – it's really not that bad without a spouse. Both scenarios have very different blessings and strengths. So I'm not putting marriage down. I'm simply stressing that you choose your future spouse DAMN carefully. If you chose to release yourself from the single life style for marriage, then make sure the new benefits of commitment out way the losses of single life. This goes for both sexes!

Should my opinions be a bit one sided, well these are based on my experiences and I'd welcome your opinions. The option to write your book is extended and no one is stopping you. Even if you never go to publish, you won't believe the therapeutic value I experienced while writing it. Not to mention what you learn about yourself, those you love and the world around you. Perhaps a high school requirement should be to write a book?

Back to stereo typing those around us. Well I don't think this will ever go away, it's a subconscious attitude that we learnt from childhood. Our parents helped this programming by encouraging us to favor certain habits, frown on certain pass times, and even prejudge according to signs we picked up from those around us.

So this is a tough one to break, but simply being aware of our flaws helps reduce the instinctive urge to doubt the intentions of our best friends, partners and strangers, especially should we feel they're taking advantage of us. This in turn will set a new standard towards your own relationship, as well as potentially improve your working environment, expand your circle of friends and more. If only we spent more time giving our friends the benefit of the doubt?

Now a friend of mine said to me 'go with your gut feel', in other words listen to your instincts! This to me goes hand in glove with a form of stereotyping the person you're about to criticize, or make a decision about. So here is what I think we should do:

1) Listen to your instincts as there's a reason for their existence, but do not act immediately should they be negative, rather take heed of the 'gut' warning and research the situation before making a decision to see if your 'warning' had merit.

2) Listen to the person in question completely before making a negative comment. (Damn, if only I learnt this a long time ago, I'd probably be a much wiser lad by now!) Okay, I do agree some people are complete idiots, but please be careful when applying this generalization.

3) The time taken to evaluate the situation is often a lot less than the time needed to repair the situation caused by lack of consideration.

Now there's no real turn on for any relationship and activating the old nymph gland than remembering how your spouse naturally assumed that you were a lazy, selfish and inconsiderate sloth! "

So here's one thing we can assume.
Not listening to your partner, or stereo typing their intentions without careful thinking can seriously create an unsensual, lack of intimacy, hostile relationship – the type of growth environment the nun gland thrives on. Best wishes for this one folks, being a normal human has one or two drawbacks.

Chapter 6: My First Wife

We first met in early our twenties; we both had the same ambitions, the same interests, the same outlook and attitude to life, to society, and thought we could make a great team. Well we at first did, it was a great idea and we started living together almost immediately. Although the cartoon below illustrates my last passing thoughts on her!

FRED, THE HAIRDRYER, NOW!

Just a quick run down of wife number one before you assume I believe she is the scum of the earth.

1) She actually has a good heart, a twisted mind, but her deluded intentions are almost noble. Although she presently believes everyone is out to get her, she once had a really strong drive to help people. During our marriage she had two distinctive characters, both complete opposites.

2) I believe her brain not to be functioning correctly, this is not her fault as she has no control of the manufacture of these chemical elements in her head, and this is why the psychiatrist made the comments you will read later. Upon my own visit several years later I learnt from a medical view how our personal characters could be lead to believe the most unrealistic circumstances as a result of imbalances within our mind beyond our control.

3) I only hold her responsible for not acknowledging the possibility of her mental illness, not the actions of them. But then perhaps this too is a result of her illness?

4) I also do think that possibly her programming, or rather formation years of her character were subjected to discomforting input. Her older siblings were already young adults when her parents began to break apart if I recall correctly? Now there is quite a range of details in the parameters of what we might deem "normal" society specifications. And we might ask who has the right to determine these specs. While she was exposed to the bickering from toddler onwards the older brother and sister already had an understanding of what was happening with their parents – just food for thought?

Then I got to learn about her, how her family always discouraged her regarding her choice of career, how they always criticized her in many of her interests. Perhaps they were right to do so to? She was also institutionalized by her parents from the age of 6 for depression as well as not following the norm as required by society. I will never forget when she told me how her dad reprimanded her feeding sugar to ants at the age of 5. She was made to feel bad for simply trying to do something good. We got closer together as a result of this. Sympathy marriages do not work! Been there, done that, got the divorce papers.

Then there were the other issues that never came to the foreground. Topics I asked her about that she never answered. I also asked her once if her dad ever abused or molested her – she simply went quiet. At the time of writing there is a court case against her with an alleged witness claiming to have seen her possibly molesting our daughter.

I also enquired why she would feel criticized by colleagues at work, why she felt everyone was out to "get her". This had manifested many years ago, before we were even married. I will also never forget the psychiatrist saying one day that she would never be cured and would need constant medication. I refused to accept this then – my mistake, but she felt secure with my support and I believed I was doing the right thing for both her and I.

I was under the misguided illusion that we, the human being, were always totally responsible for our own actions and always in total control regarding our observations and decisions. I didn't then understand the complexity of the physical working of the human brain. (Not that I claim to be the expert now!)

Then after getting married less than a year later - an attempted suicide by her, and a termination – she refused to have our first child! Just quickly folks, abortions suck! I still feel guilty for siding with her on that decision, I feel as if I signed that child's death certificate. Unless the child is going to be still born, have 5 legs and no arms or an unpronounceable disease, please think twice before you consider this option.

As for the suicide attempt? She disappeared from work after being employed for 3 months due to her colleagues picking on her and apparently questioning her approach to the business. I found out later there was a pattern regarding this as she seldom held down a steady job for more than 6 months. The result of the suicide attempt was a stomach pump, and a few weeks at a mental clinic. This is where the said psychiatrist informed me of her need for permanent medication.

It's quite weird how someone's pain can draw you closer to them, for me I wanted to help, for her it was someone who believed in her. The suicide attempt bought us closer, and we eventually signed our commitment of "for better or worse", at the alter. After the marriage she fell pregnant again and we had a daughter. Even this pregnancy had its bumps. Big bumps!

At first she wanted to put her up for adoption, then later decided to keep her – even though unplanned our daughter was a blessing. (I think it's important to mention here that she has a record of attempted suicide from early school age – my ex-wife, not my daughter. Her wrist still looks like a map of Mars! The above-mentioned termination was her second.) The previous was apparently a friend who raped her that never went to court if I was informed correctly.

A quick trip back to the nymph to nun topic:
1) Before daughter – great sex life.
2) During pregnancy – minimal.
3) After birth – what is sex?

Now when life got more complicated with greater responsibilities, all the criticizing of her family and friends (as few as they were – her friends were becoming fewer and fewer as she claimed they were becoming more critical of her actions.) became focused on me, now I was to blame for her situation. By now she had isolated herself from almost everyone but her own mom. She often went on how were it was her father's fault for many of her families and her personal problems.

Before she blamed everyone else for her situation and she fazed them out of her life I was the only one left to blame. She was later again institutionalized after throwing plates and other crockery in front of me and our daughter and threatening to run away. I went for help at our local mental institute and she ended up in a clinic for several weeks at their recommendation, not mine. Her ranting insured her a room in maximum security in the clinic.

What I later learnt from her was that her dad recommended that she marry me for security, I had a stable job and a nice house, medical aid, a car, furniture, etc. Now there's reason and grounds for a happy marriage? Was I her soul mate or an escape from her situation? Well seeing as the odds of me meeting my soul mate is about 1 in how many billion? Unless all of us have several options or rather soul mates, which greatly increases the odds of meeting one! *See later in the book..*

A quick interjection about her father:

Her dad was a priest turned psychologist after he was persuaded to change career by the church (Assuming my ex-wife is correct) after divorcing and marrying a much younger blonde 3 months later. Mmm, the plot thickens, I never did get to hear the full story there, but I'm sure it's grounds for a great soapy. I believe they're divorced again and now he's with wife number three – a great role model for any western family?

A basic summary of this woman:

1) Constantly tried to commit suicide since early childhood.
2) Quit school after deciding not to write exams after listening to Pink Floyd.
3) Had two terminations, one was from an apparent rape by her friend? I honestly do not know truth here either.
4) Was in and out of institutions and mental clinics since age 6years.
5) Was often on medication for depression.
6) Often claimed that people were out to get her.
7) Walked out on several jobs if hint of criticism occurred – claims no one appreciated her.
8) Once disappeared, she was later found hiding in the local cemetery!
9) Now claims a direct link with God who she believes condones every action and decision she makes!
10) Now our child, at the age of 14 dreams of becoming an Israeli soldier, enjoys inflicting pain on herself, and has one "true" friend – her mom!

Now point 5 is a favorite topic of mine reinforcing my computer theory, to be explained during the book at length. If we are free souls with our own essence and logic, why do we malfunction as a result of a chemical imbalance, hence depression?

It seems to me that our existence could be the result of awareness of ourselves and a highly intricate programming allowing us "free" thought up to a point, provided our chemicals allow us to function as normal humans. Sort of like an advanced interactive PC program, as long as the hardware is stable, power supply secure, the software can function and be allowed to do it's tasks and make correct calculations. Screw with the voltage, don't provide enough RAM, introduce a virus, or disconnect a hard drive and everything falls apart.

Same with the human brain, if it's deprived of a certain chemical, given too much alcohol or drugs, we can suddenly find this free standing spirit may become depressed, randy, angry, cynical, whatever. The mind then ends up making decisions and conclusions it would never come to under "normal" situations. I can't but help wonder to what point we cross over from human to machine?

Now here's some sound personal advice to both sexes.

1) If your spouse to be has any mental illnesses please make sure they're willing to acknowledge this and be treated professionally according to the problem. Speak to a doctor. Marriage might aggravate the situation and break both your hearts eventually. Mental illness in my opinion is not an embarrassment, it's like having a physical problem, well in many cases mental illnesses are a result of a physical imbalance – just make sure it's being monitored and treated.

2) Never marry because your folks, family or friends think it's a good idea. This WILL back fire eventually, trust me. It's bad enough many of us do a career chosen, or rather "pressurized into" by our parents with the result of lack of satisfaction in our bread winning years!

3) Don't have casual sex while unprotected. The 1 + 1 = 3 formula normally causes the new addition to suffer the most. I haven't seen or been able to tell my daughter I love her for almost two years while writing this book. Every day I look at a dated photo of her and almost burst into tears, I do not wish this experience on anyone, not even a politician.

4) Never marry because you're in love with the idea of being in love. Neither marry because you feel sorry for them and believe in them. You can believe in some one without marriage. No

50

matter how much you love some one, make sure they love you too and their motivations for marriage are as sincere as yours.

5) Be prepared that there is a really high percentage of probability that your intimacy and sex will decline rapidly after conception in many cases, and get worse after birth. I wish more people would realize the benefits of sex and not think that some one who enjoys it is a pervert. Next time in a shop please look at the magazine shelf and see how many magazines feature why sex is good for us, not just men!

So what happened to my ex wife? Well she now holds me solely responsible for our failed marriage. I do admit we both made huge mistakes while under influence of too much alcohol and I'm paying the price too. But when will she take responsibility for her affair (yep, we're both guilty of this one), admit that giving your underwear away at functions is not cool, and also admit to liters of intake of the dreaded but most enjoyed liquids, yeah she also had many a hangover!

After our separation up until about 9months after our divorce we got on really well in separate homes. Then I met my second wife, the complete opposite of number1. She won over our daughter within minutes, made me incredibly happy, and enjoyed life and people. My daughter made her a gift or two, told mommy how wonderful dad's new girl friend was, and then guess what happened? The ex-wife simply packed up and disappeared to stay with her sister, about 1100kms away!

I later learnt that her sister commented on her attitude to my daughter's education, or rather lack of it, which resulted in them moving again, to stay with her dad. This also caused conflict and she moved into what we might consider just a tiny bit more up market than a public toilet in a town lost in time. Here she could avoid any conflicts from family and neighbors.

Imagine this home. Sand for a garden, broken fencing, wasp nest outside the front door (with relevant stings on occasion), spiders treated as pets, a lamb walking around the inside home (I'm not kidding – he's name was Lammertjie), paint falling off walls, a bed that looked pre 1914, had to boil water to run a bath, the mattress was almost collapsed, and more.. This I learnt before she moved back to Cape Town.

She also led me to believe our daughter's education was on track. When they again moved to Cape Town I found out the contrary. My daughter's sight had deteriated too and she needs glasses. (Spectacles) She had only received education in subjects that her mom had deemed okay by her exclusive link to God! She now claims divine communication giving her the ultimate truth regarding her care giving responsibilities.

She has also begun a court case against me for never paying maintenance for our child – which is not true; I have all receipts to prove otherwise. She claims I have several cars – I have a 12year old dented car. She also believes I have a R45000 overdraft, while in reality my credit card was cancelled by the bank due to lack of funds.

Now the court initially believed her story and even though I've asked them to consult her medical records providing them with contact names, and places - they refused to do so! Bear in mind that they offered to help me at first, and asked me to provide them with details regarding the ex-wife's history. So much for placing my faith in the South African judicial system!

As mentioned, my daughter, now 14 wants to become an Israeli soldier, she enjoys inflicting pain on herself and believes that I know longer wish to care or provide for her. She has become the ex wife's pawn in a sick attempt for her to hurt me. For all you out there that have split paths with your spouse, please don't use your children to inflict misery. They actually lose more than we do.

To wife number1: Well-done – you have hurt me just like you promised to, but at the unfair expense of our little girl – well done!

But as mentioned at the beginning, perhaps her distorted reality allows her an excuse to justify her means. If she's a victim of her bodies own malfunction, how can I blame her? Her fault is to not acknowledge or entertain the thought of her having an illness, but if her programming doesn't allow for this due to a physical problem, who steps in? When I mentioned this to the prosecutor, they simply did nothing. Although the family advocate now has a case to research her well being initiated by me for my child's sake.

Perhaps this is the beginning of my opinion that the state is too slack, and/or lazy, if they had done the research I requested of them almost 20months ago, they would of discovered these truths and they could of drawn to an accurate conclusion over a year ago instead of subjecting my child to her faulty mother for so many more months.

Maybe their spouses (the State's) are too busy flying around in unauthorized plane trips. I trust you read the scandal late 2005 about a family joy ride by one of our politicians family enjoying our national aircraft– the guilty party had to pay for it, if not found out it would have been our tax money funding these people. I wonder if they ever did repay this, did we ever see the cheque and receipt? Mmm, we can only wonder!

Time line comments:
I've resumed writing after a 7month break to try and be more objective and slightly less emotional. The family advocate called me asking me if I had my ex-wife's details, they cannot get in contact with her. So she's running again, but this time with my child. The court knows of my limited contact ability with my child, so if they cannot reach her, how can I help?

The initial court case was thrown out as my ex-wife failed to prove her claims regarding my millions she believes I am earning, my several cars she said I owned, her being unable to validate her statement that a previous magistrate lied, and much more. She didn't even arrive for the last hearing, the state seemed to accept this but when I almost had a nervous breakdown they asked for a second opinion? This whole exercise cost me in excess of R80000 to simply prove that I did try my best and did not intend to get retrenched.

The irony is now that my situation has improved the extra income pays my legal fees – this could have been extra income for my daughter and my present family. The worst part for is the State PROMISING me assistance, then doing NOTHING, and I am in debt due to their lack of commitment. I must contribute tax to pay for these people's salaries? Where is the justice!

Chapter 7: My Second Wife

Being a glutton for punishment I decided to exchange my newfound freedom for another relationship and commitment. About 9months after being officially and legally rid of my first soul mate I met my second. I wonder if the 9month period could liken to a new birth of an era in my life? I'm sure some people who enjoy attaching a form of symbolism might entertain this thought.

It's actually quite interesting how loyal human nature is, it simply switches loyalties. Now before you comment on my fast rebound, at least I met my new partner after being divorced. (Unlike my ex wife's dad - and we were separated for over a year too.)

Hey I should have been a Zulu or other African tribal member. I could simply accumulate wives as I went along. Although I thought Mbeki (our noble president) said we were all equal, so does that mean that I can also as a white male have several wives? I mean, we're no longer allowed to attach racial preference anymore? If not, isn't this some sort of racial discrimination? Let's not open more worms yet.

Now before some of my initial comments suggest that I do not wish to be with wife number two, let me quickly some up my feelings for her:

1) She is wonderful, warm, friendly, caring, loving, this is what attracted me to her, just like many of your partners were in your opinion when meeting them.

2) She makes me both happy and frustrated, just like I'm sure I attract the same response from her. The trick is not to dwell too long on our spouse's negative side – no, you're not perfect either! If only we could ask ourselves this question every time

before entering into an argument, "Will the outcome of this debate be positive or negative, would it be better to overlook small problems as a form of compromise?"

3) Although her methods some times defy all MALE logic, the motivations behind her actions are often for my good too. Ask yourself what the long-term goal is behind your spouse, you might be pleasantly surprised. Now ask yourself if your habits don't convert a few of her hairs to gray too?

I must share our first encounter. Believe it or not I'm really extremely shy around women and when I was performing in my band and I saw my "wife to be" for the first time I was so scared of rejection that I decided to avoid her. It was her that approached me and offered me a schnapps!

So we were off to a good first start, at least I knew I wasn't going to be turned away. Later the evening she asked what I did as a career. (It's amazing how many people don't see performing music as a career.) So I explained that I also teach music to which she replied, "Oh, I suppose you must be gay!" My response was "Well why not take me home and find out?" She did! Six years later we're still going well with a wonderful little boy who is not 6years minus 9months old. He turns 5 May 2006.

Once more it's interesting how certain career options are stereo typed, for example, are so many music teachers gay? Most male teachers I know are married to the opposite sex too. They also have no desire to be in the "shit" either as one can expect to be in a gay male relationship. (Hey, if you cannot laugh at yourselves or your values than it's quite sad, this goes for both the "straight" and the gays out there.) It's sort of like how politicians are branded as professional liars and thieves in most jokes and cartoons. (Well at least there's truth in that one?)

Now when I met number two we had a sex life to die for, the nymph gland was strong and healthy. She initiated the deed as much as I did. I even had my first blowjob while driving the car when returning from friends. Yep, I had finally arrived, everything I wanted to believe about women was confirmed, here I had a beautiful woman that actually enjoyed and wanted to have sex with ME!

Then one day a successful sperm beat the other few million to it's future home and decided to begin growing after initiating fertilization, the 9-month transition kicked in. The nymph gland got moved to the darkest biological corner and our sex life began its rather quick downward spiral. Not only did this avenue change, the female hormone started running erratic once more.

Quick advice! Never, ever, cross a pregnant woman! Do not make her angry or question her judgment, do so at your own peril! Mood swings were the call of the day. Why on earth would a loving God program a woman's biological hormones to react in such a manner? Nothing really good comes from it!

Although some argue it prepares you for the sleepless nights with an infant in the house. I'm not quite in agreement here; I would think we need extra good memories leading up to the tiring yet rewarding experience of child raising. I've personally found that good memories help us through bad times, so to build up more stress before delivery date doesn't make sense. What do you think?

Well we made it through with a few hectic bumps and our gift was delivered through large belly cut that looked like a nightmare on a butcher's table. (Never seen a caesarian while the doctors delivering a child? It's a beautiful unnerving experience, amazing but the amount of blood is not for the weak!) Now we were three. And the sincerest thank you to the doctors for all the training to do this so painlessly!

We felt stronger and tied together through this experience of being able to contribute to the human life cycle. Other side effects from this are lack of sleep, tiredness, irritableness, and the "nun" gland now taking its position more seriously. Unfortunately the male hormones react quite differently to those of the woman.

It seems that Mother Nature really didn't design many woman for sex after birth. (I'm not talking about the first few hours idiot, I mean the next few months!) Ever notice how many articles are written in magazines regarding women who now no longer feel like sex with reasons like "I'm too fat", or "I've got stretch marks". Other favorites are "I'm too tired" and the list grows. (The last is quite valid, I was pretty exhausted too, but really contented with our wonderful son. Although I missed the physical relationship now becoming a faded memory, the joy my son bought was incredible.

Now for some or other reason, the male, who should be (and often is, believe it or not) equally as exhausted still has this urge to enjoy the exchange of body fluids. So here human instinct verses human logic and emotions start to bend under conflict of interests!

If society allowed the concubine theory there'd be no problem, see chapter10. The other wives, and/or concubines could both help the new mother and the dad could keep his natural programming under control too. It would be a winning situation for all, but then our legal profession's main money-spinner would lose too much of their revenue. Interesting though for a conspiracy theory don't you think?

Another sad fact is the amount of articles I've read where woman feel guilty for their lack of sex drive. This proves my theory that we are nothing more than a complex program (with some serious defects) with an awareness factor. To validate this, the woman knows she doesn't want to have sex but the self-awareness factor conflicts with the program creating confusion and frustration. If we were really the free spirit we like to claim to be, surely we could work our way around this challenge and do what we believe is correct and follow our biological design?

This can almost be compared to alcohol or drugs, for example. We end up doing things we know are wrong, but we find it difficult to resist, almost impossible. Our entire character and morals standards can be influenced by a physical entity. So where is the separation between spiritual and physical?

I've seen this proven in many situations where my wife, myself, friends and acquaintances all act completely out of character when affected by a substance of sorts. Even tiredness can cause us to act irrationally, so are we really human or a machine of unique design?

With animals we refer to instinct, this I believe to be their individual program. The upright, pink mammal called homosapien prefers to think they are exempt from this. I'd love to hear some medical and philosophical views on this. We have the audacity to think we're actually in complete control of our own life! Yep, that's why we succumb to drugs, alcohol, develop bad habits & routines, have affairs, resign our selves to television, fail to stand up to bullies and so much more. We want to escape!

Why try and escape something if you have ability to change it. Are you really that in control of your life? (Just for the record I do NOT encourage drugs, neither have I used them, but I do enjoy a drink and I am guilty of have an ale too many on occasion.)

Well back to wife number two. Yeah we have a few set backs that I'm sure are not unique to our relationship – see the chapter on pets. I often wonder why she married me, she says she does love me, well I love her too. But maybe this is as a person loves a dear friend, not as a soul mate? Perhaps our admiration for a really wonderful person coupled with good looks (She does have amazing breasts too) causes us to get confused with love?

I have also begun to doubt the existence of soul mates. Perhaps this is a romantic illusion to make the situation we find ourselves in a little better – a form of justification for pairing up. Think about it folks, there's billions of us strolling around this planet, some with more direction than others. So what is the percentage odds that your soul mate will happen to come into your life just at that right mystical, magical time when both of you are ready to find each other? I trust the law of averages on this one to prove it's way under 0.0001%. Yet so many claim this, and later divorce?

If we look at a few thousand years ago I recall that many husbands and wives didn't share the same tent – the result? Look for the word divorce in the bible or any similar books – it's not there! I also believe some Eastern practices subscribe to this with similar results.

I must be honest and say that some of the best times I've had were during the year of separation and the 9 months between wife number one and wife number two! I had 21months of "freedom".

My present wife initially inspired this book, although she has no idea I'm writing it. The inspiration to write was reinforced when I found that many male friends felt the same as I did towards their spouse. They loved them, but were frustrated with the active nun gland.

They also often got tired of lack of direction and simply co existing with their partner from day to day – see chapter on careers for a solution. Not to mention my comments on TV. (Again, I do stress that I truly believe that many women have the equally frustrating comments as to how they must tolerate the 'willy' carriers on earth. – So come on ladies, let the boys learn how you see things.)

Please people, I'm not knocking marriage or women, I'm simply commenting on my observations based on my personal life and that of many friends. The object of this book is to help share and understand how life impacts both of us. We need to know who or what we are. We need to take responsibility for our lives and not be so complacent. I think that too many divorces are the result of these facts:

1) We rely on our partner for purpose in life, to make us happy. Charity starts at home people, you must be happy with yourself first.

2) We refuse to acknowledge that there is some sort of biological program running in our body that only too often distorts reality as perceived by the brain.

3) TV promotes laziness, and a too easy excuse to do nothing. You are not "busy" watching TV. You're often choosing to be

a spectator, and trying to escape your life's problems by living into another, you're not "busy".

Now let me explain my present living conditions. We are lucky to have a small built on flatlet onto the main house. This is my home; it has a small lounge, a bathroom and one bedroom where I rest my head. While my wife resigned herself to the TV I wrote this book, listen to music, enjoyed the peace and tranquility of my fish and cats. I also compose, teach, and program my software from this home in a home. The results are great. I'm not forced to be exposed to TV's offering. When my wife and I do share a bed it's really special. We have space! Since adopting this living arrangement we no longer fight nearly as often. (Probably less than 90% of previous run-ins and stress.)

When we shared a bed and tried to do too much together we fought consistently. About the TV, dogs, hers and my friends coming and going when the other wanted space, the list was endless. Now she has her hobbies, which keep her happy, we don't feel obliged to entertain each other's friends, and she can get happiness from her environment. When she's happy, it makes my world happier too, and vice versa. She gets to share her contentment with me, not compromising and stress as these have been avoided.

Even though it's not separate tents as a few thousand years ago, it has similar parallels.

The lesson to be learnt here:
Do not to try and change some one, my wife has some wonderful attributes, and I'd not like her to lose these, that would be losing her essence. The problem with trying to convince or convert some one to your way of thinking is that you might come across as bullying, pushy and also give your partner the feeling of inadequacy. If you succeed in changing them, you also lose the person you initially fell in love with, is this a good thing?

Rather live your life to your own ideals, if they're really that good there's a better chance of your spouse seeing the success and following an example as opposed to feeling pushed into something. There must have been some thing good for you and your partner to marry, focus on this and not the negative. Water something and it grows.

The happiness that our child is surrounded with from his mom and dad makes the whole relationship more than worth it for me. To see him laugh and smile and enjoy life is the ultimate reward for me. Remember, no child requested to be here, they here as a result of our lusts and/or biological needs.

The fact that wife number one has removed my first child from me is a tragedy for all concerned. For those contemplating divorce, don't use your children as leverage – it's sick and simply WRONG! Obviously if one parent is a pedophile remove the child, or if there's a clinical illness get medical advice. But if it's simply clash of characters, don't be so pathetic!

So it's our duty to lead them to learn, not dictate to them to become morons without questioning. This always backfires later. Ever notice how many serial killers, rapists, etc. come from dysfunctional homes? Coincidence – I don't think so!

To summarize, life with wife number is really quite neat. I'm truly grateful to her wonderful attributes and apologize for some times focusing on her weaknesses. She's given me a stunning home, the most beautiful child, cares for me, and encourages me to pursue my interests in both career and hobby. So to condemn her for an inactive nymph gland is not really fair.

I have so much more with her than others do from their partner that still enjoy sex. So every time that I feel horny may I quickly consult with my hand, get rid of the hormonal build up and be grateful for what I have, not for what is missing.

Who knows what tomorrow might bring?

Time line comments:

Well, it's been a long time, wife number 2 knows about the book, it's content, and supports it even though she has not yet read it. The past few weeks have lead us to rediscover each other, which is really great. It's almost like meeting her again, but still with active nun gland, but now she's addressing the issue and IS trying really hard to revive the nymph inside her.

On the whole, I wouldn't swap her for any one, well maybe Sandra Bullock, but I think my wife's future is secure! (Just kidding people) I also presently feel optimistic about the future, and trying to predict it is simply not worth the effort. We have the NOW to build, and this in turn will help supply strength through troubles to come.

CHAPTER 8: DIVORCE, THE FINAL FRONTIER

Sort of symbolic the comparison between Star Trek's claim of: "Space the final frontier"? Isn't one of the many excuses for divorce the need to find 'space', and as for it being 'final'? Some might argue it's just the opening to a whole new universe which still spins around one's ex-spouse in many cases, read the chapter about wife #1? So we can learn from sci-fi movies – see ch18 on TV.

Now divorce isn't always a bad thing, it has many hidden blessings, especially when one of the two partners is deranged, a bully, or simply just a jerk! But too often it serves as an easy way out when the going gets tough, or when our own animal lusts favor a new direction and simply too lazy to nurture their present relationship.

I'm sure we can think of dozens of valid and lame excuses to make this decision. The saddest part is those who have no control over the loss of a family and often one parent – this person is? You guessed it, the CHILD!

I guess to write reasons and guidelines of when a divorce is the answer vs how to save a failing marriage is a book on it's own. And a damn big one at that!

Now some quick statistics: It has been proven that every divorce started with a marriage! (One of the few stats that cannot be argued?) So the clue lies in who we marry and the reasons to motivate this commitment. In a perfect world we need not ever experience break-up, but reality brings us to be confronted with countless unpleasant issues that raise debate, arguments, conflicts, distractions and temptations. So we need tools to deal with fixing and maintaining our relationships.

Once more I think the clue lies in whom we chose. Western society certainly has too many standards imposed on them via media exposure, political systems, economic stresses, environmental conditions and racial backgrounds. So when you consider sharing your life with another it's a really good idea if you both at least share a common ground on most, if not all of these issues.

On media standards: How many women feel they must live up to the "babe" in the advert on TV that most of males drool over? Yeah lads – we must make sure of our opinions here, it can hurt our spouses. And for the ladies, please don't always think on our behalf, lots of us men are sincerely happy with our partners and have no issues with how you look.

As for me, I think too many models on TV are just too thin, have no tits, and actually quite boring, my wife is awesome, if only she believed me. This approach is surprisingly shared by more men regarding their spouses' attributes than you might think! So if maybe your husband does think of you as sex kitten as well as his partner, is that so bad?

Political systems: If we have conflicts on this we start comparing moral standards and issues too, as well as worrying about the future of the country we live in. As we're faced with political debates daily on the news both on TV and radio as well as the newspapers, magazines and more, there's going to be voiced differences here.

Economic stresses: This can be internal – within the family, or external - simply the cost of living and the standards there-of expected by each partner. Make sure before sign your life away at the alter that you both have the means to attain your combined goals, and more importantly, that you share that similar goals! And most importantly, share the same understanding should you not achieve them! Blame shifting failure on to your spouse is rarely fair. (Unless the one is an idiot – get to know your partner before you commit to them people!)

Environment conditions: I guess this one ties in largely with political issues in many instances. But depending on your hobbies, choosing to live in a country or area to make one spouse happy can have a negative impact on the other. Imagine a city person nobly sacrificing them self so their spouse can live on a farm. Unless both partners enjoy the attributes that come with certain living environments and conditions, there's bound to be conflict later, we can only sacrifice up to a point! It's not rocket science folks, we're just human.

Racial backgrounds: Now this might not mean black and white! It could be cultural background too. For example a German marrying a Japanese could possibly have some stressful implications. They both have a very different tradition and background. Not that either of these cultures are wrong, neither is any other culture! It just takes a lot of effort depending on the INDIVIDUALS involved in this and any other relationship. Perhaps the above example relationship has been tried and tested successfully many times?

We're all individuals, but the key lies in thinking before you act. Be honest with yourself and your partner. Make sure that compromising from both parties are kept at a minimum, and don't rush love. Didn't Phil Collins sing, "You can't hurry love"? Listen to this song; it has a wealth of hints and tips for relationships.

Here are some solutions to avoid your children's tears, and a few car installments for a divorce attorney:

1) **Talking to each other**: This is arguably the most important tool to build a relationship. Don't ever be too tired or say "later dear, after the TV program or sports show". This just makes the other feel worthless.

2) **Listen to each other:** I know this sounds too obvious, but dividing your attention between your spouse and something else is NOT a cool idea. I've been caught out here too, and I think you might be lying should you say this temptation never became a reality to you!

3) **Plan with each other:** Make a common goal, something you both really enjoy or want out of life. There is very little that a

couple cannot do if they get their 'game plan' on paper with a lot of thought. The success both partners can experience at completion of the task or event will definitely help the nymph gland grow from strength to strength.

4) **Make time for each other:** We all want some time apart and together, the problem occurs when the one mammal wants it's together time when the other needs to be alone. Perhaps point 3 about planning could sort this out? Either way, being alone at times is life preservingly important! Let your partner have this space and don't think they no longer love you when they take it. If you need a hug so often and have to have some one adoring you 24/7, get a dog!

5) **Think before you act:** Another obvious one folks! Bear in mind that most humans, your spouse being part of that species, are really quite nice. So when they're down, irritable or just tired, try and understand that maybe they had a bad day at work; maybe they're ill, or worried about the future in their country. The list of possible concerns is endless.

6) **Share you worry**: This goes hand-in-glove with point 5. Your partner cannot smell why you're down; you do owe it to them to tell them what your concerns are. Keep in mind that most likely your partner wants you to be happy, and they probably worried when you're down or quiet. And it's only natural to think that they might be the cause of it without them necessarily being guilty of some thing. At least assure them it's not them and that it could it be work, illness, or an outside facture that has you troubled but you don't wish to talk about yet.

Divorce is often a breakup that should have taken place years ago before the marriage! The parting of paths that could have been done a lot more pleasantly, or at least with a lot less hostility should it have taken place during the dating period.

We might be saving ourselves when divorcing, but we could be breaking the world of a young child or children, who is often exposed to emotional blackmail, losing a parent, and being set a real lousy set of standards regarding family values. We need to realize that children look to us for guidance; we have a huge responsibility to them, which should be exciting, wonderful, and a blessing.

If only so many people had faith in themselves, if we could make ourselves happy and not rely on others for this. If we believed in our own capabilities in finding that 'perfect' partner and didn't resign ourselves to the "better the devil you know" scenario.

We need to conquer our fear of loneliness and find peace within ourselves. Then we'd probably be able to make much better relationship choices, and therefore reduce the statistics of divorced people.

So before we have to see divorce as the last resource, please realize the implications of choosing a partner that might not be ideal in the long term. Compromising too much is eventually going to lead to down fall. This won't help you or them. Sometimes being selfish is a good thing. Find happiness in yourself, if your spouse does the same and chooses to share the walk through life with you there's bound to be a greater chance of a wonderful marriage, family and future. It is possible.

Prevention IS better than cure!

Chapter 9: Divorced Wives

Ever read the 'singles corner' in many magazines, the ever growing section where you find the following type of advert:
"Blue eyes from Bloemfontein, 1.6m, 54kg, 1 dependent, likes dancing, occasional drink. Looking for independent man who doesn't smoke"

Scary that we can be reduced to this type of advertising? I've yet to meet anyone who has tried this method of mating with good results, but I'm sure they're there. Now what is this woman saying? Let's have some fun analyzing this:

1) Blues eyes – normally associated with beauty, so she's hinting that she has stunning eyes, or at least she has some pleasing attributes.

2) 1.6m – she's not too tall, maybe trying to convey she might be petite.

3) 54kg – she is saying, "I'm not fat!" but possibly quite sexy or at least appealing, so there's the nymph gland pointing out an attractive feature like bait for her next spouse. I wonder if the weight listed is the truth here though, maybe she's actually 68kg, but tries to look thinner when squeezing into a pair of jeans 2 sizes to small for her?

4) 1 dependant – well we know she's not a virgin now, so she does have sex, or did at least once! She might also be advertising for a father for her child, so be careful!

5) Likes dancing & occasional drink – enjoys more of a home life but tolerates parties. Now how many are going to honest and say, I love getting sozzled! Or that they're complete party

animals. Similarly very few might want to meet some one who has no ambition and simply want to watch TV without financial stresses. Still no real clues here?

6) Independent man – in other words a man who is financially well off or at least stable, so what they really want is money to bail them out of their probably sad state of affairs they've found themselves in. They should just be honest and adjust the advert to say "Looking for wealthy male to support me, and I'm not too ugly to have as an accessory. I might also have intercourse with you to help you accept me better. Lastly, I only have one child who needs a father figure."

The above comments are honestly tongue in cheek and the advert is fictitious, but it goes to show how we could possibly "read into" and translate an innocent, honest, yet sad method of searching for the right partner.

Not that I should talk, I was equally keen on pairing up again when meeting my new wife, was this the male equivalent of the nymph gland or my smaller brain saying "go boy, go"? I must admit the sex at first encounters was, and I use the word WAS, really great. Now be honest both species, does, or did sex play an important part of your life at first?

Although Western Christian society frowns upon premarital sex, it is gradually becoming a way of life and I dare to say that there are many more unmarried, or rather 'never been married' non-virgins walking around now than there were a hundred years ago. This life style change has merits and pitfalls. Like most things in life, take your time, don't rush and use in moderation.

There also seems to be ulterior motives for many divorced woman to find a new partner. Sex plays an important role for many of these women. As men really enjoy sex, what better way to ensure a man by leading him to believe he's found that nymph he's dreamt of? After marriage we're back to the title of this book.

Perhaps a quick look at the humor in this email might explain what men and woman would expect from each other in an ideal world. I must admit that from a chauvinist view I've certainly seen worse suggestions!

THE PERFECT DAY - FOR HER

8.15 Wake up to hugs and kisses.

8.30 Weigh in 2Kg lighter than yesterday.

8.45 Breakfast in bed, freshly squeezed orange juice and croissants - open presents - expensive jewellery chosen by thoughtful partner.

9.15 Soothing hot bath with frangipani bath oil.

10.00 Light work out at club with sexy funny personal trainer! 10.30 Facial, manicure, shampoo, condition, blow dry.

12.00 Lunch with best friend at fashionable outdoor cafe.

12.45 Catch sight of partner's ex and notices she has gained 17kg.

1.00 Shopping with friends, unlimited credit.

3.00 Nap.

4.00 Three dozen roses delivered by florist, card is from secret admirer.

4.15 Light work out at club, followed by massage from strong but gentle hunk, who says he rarely gets to work on such a perfect body

5.30 Choose outfit from expensive designer wardrobe, parade before full-length mirror.

7.30 Candle lit dinner for two followed by dancing, with compliments received from other diners/dancers.

10.00 Hot shower (alone).

10:50 Carried to bed . . . (freshly ironed, crisp, new, white linen).

11.00 Pillow talk, light touching and cuddling.

11.15 Fall asleep in his big strong arms.

THE PERFECT DAY - FOR HIM

6.00 Alarm.

6.15 Blow job.

6.30 Massive satisfying shit while reading the sports section.

7.00 Breakfast: rump steak and eggs, coffee and toast, all cooked by naked, buxom wench who bends over a lot showing her growler

7.30 Limo arrives.

7.45 Several Beers en-route to airport.

9.15 Flight in personal Lear Jet.

9.30 Limo to Mirage Resort Golf Club (blow job en-route).

9.45 Play front nine - 2 under.

11.45 Lunch - Pie, chips and gravy, 3 lagers and a bottle of Dom Perignon.

12.15 Blow job.

12.30 Play back nine - 4 under.

2.15 Limo back to the airport (Several Bourbons).

2.30 Fly to Cairns.

3.30 Late afternoon fishing excursion with all female crew, all nude who also bend over a lot displaying growlers.

4.30 Land world record Marlin (1234lbs) - on light tackle.

5.00 Fly home, massage and hand job by naked Elle McPherson (bending over.... naturally).

6.45 Shit, Shower and Shave.

7.00 Watch news: Michael Jackson assassinated; cannabis legalized.

7.30 Dinner: lobster appetizers, Dom Perignon (1953), big juicy fillet steak followed by Ice-cream served on a big pair of tits.

9.00 Napoleon Brandy and Habanos cigar in front of wall-size TV as you watch match of the day; Swindon beating Oxford Utd by 4-0

9.30 Sex with three women (all with lesbian tendencies...some bending over).

11.00 Massage and Jacuzzi with tasty pizza snacks and a cleansing ale.

11.30 A nightcap blowjob.

11.45 In bed alone.

11.50 A 22 second fart which changes note 4 times and forces the dog to leave the room.

11.51 Laugh yourself to sleep!!

With so many different expectations from each other, is it such a surprise that so many divorced people walk this earth? But seriously, the above words might not be so far removed from the truth. So I guess there's a lot of compromise from both sexes to be exercised before marriage nirvana can be reached.

The fact that so many 'singles wanted' adverts as mentioned previously exist validates the human drive to find contentment in someone instead of them selves or something. It is so much easier to rely on someone else instead of finding purpose within. I believe mankind really needs to be aware of the stress implications regarding this and reprogram their way of thinking. Once more, ever notice how we like being around happy people? This is because that the happy person has more than likely found joy and fulfillment within them self, and the spectator wants a slice of it.

Learn from this folks.

Time line comments:
Well I've survived another 6-7months without adding to the population of divorced women I'm really glad to say. In fact things are getting better gradually in many aspects, not all, but many, and this is a good thing! So it doesn't look like I'll be reading the partner wanted column (Unless my morning shit needs some motivation and/or I need a giggle), or paying a few installments on an attorney's new car.

My wife and I are settling into a better than comfortable relationship with each other with good reason for more optimistic improvements in other sections of our lives. Maybe her nymph gland will come to life again one day before my willy forgets it's pleasurable side. But I'm sure a good hand massage will relieve the hormonal stress linked with celibacy.

Divorce is never cool, and statistics prove that every divorce has started with marriage (duh!) But seriously, be bluddy careful before taking this road, breaking up really hurts every one, both those in the right and the wrong…

To the divorced men and women I offer the following. Bear in mind I'm one of them! Learn from past commitments; think carefully about who you are and what you want. Find internal peace and contentment, hobbies normally help, and they introduce you to people that share the same interests. (Not a bad place to meet your next partner?) Hobbies also help create an escape from daily chores.

Chapter 10: The Concubine Theory

Scientists believe that only dolphins and humans have intercourse for fun. I wonder how they asked the dolphins? As for dogs, they seem to hump almost anything; it's hard to believe they don't enjoy this judging by their expression! Then again, I'm not the expert.

Now many couples, like our aquatic mammal counterpart, start off having fun, enjoying doing things together which often includes having sex! We'll be looking at how this changes with marriage and offer some practical solutions.

With most my friends and their girl friends as well as myself in the past, we enjoyed physical relationships as well as an active social one. (Although churches frown at premarital sex, the diminishing amount of virgins at the alter nowadays seems to hint at our lack of moral convictions from religion.) We all used to go out, have fun, entertain guests, and enjoy hobbies. Then one day, normally after marriage a family is planned, or just happens!

Now please do not think I'm trying to discourage a family, I would never think of changing history at all if it meant the fruit of our loins would cease to exist. I cannot imagine life without my son and daughter. The sad thing is that many love their children so much they try almost anything to keep the marriage alive so that the children can have a happy wonderful home where their parent suppress all attempts of killing each other.

(When a couple gets together they enjoy sex anywhere, after marriage it seems to only occur in the passage. We look over our shoulder as our spouse

edges past and mumble 'fuck you!' – bad humor, sorry)

It seems that once our lover turns to mother they often get this insane insecure feeling that their husbands no longer find them attractive. This is really weird, they just gave birth to a combined flesh and blood living soul and they think their partners won't think they (The mothers) are wonderful and attractive and even more special. Many also make the error of generalizing and forgetting that we're all individuals.

Yes there are many idiot males who don't appreciate the gift their spouse has given them and the pain and efforts they've gone through. Similarly there's many woman who feel they're now too fat, too tired, or forget they have husbands who still believe them to be wonderful and now even more attractive. And the husband has to live with this and understand the change in their nature.

So who really has it worse?
Here's a tough one as many feel that they're the victim and their spouse isn't trying hard enough or doesn't know the pain, stress and anguish they're going through. Well seeing as this is MY book and these opinions are based on what I know and have been exposed to, and the invite has been extended for others to write their side of the story – which I sincerely hope they do to help us all understand the human race, it's need to procreate, the need to provide and succeed, etc.. I really hope for a sequence to this book to feature the comments and new truths that have been shared with me, remember that the purpose of this book is meant to be a learning curve to help both sexes understand each other.

Please bear in mind that each of us has learnt and been exposed to something that the other more than likely hasn't, and that the experience and information interchanging might help us understand and grow in our walk on mother earth. Sharing also provides healthy and interesting topics for discussion.

My purpose on this blue planet as I see it, is to provide for my spawn, love my mate and also enjoy my short visit, personally I also have a strong desire for success, a feeling of accomplishment.

I'm not going to debate reincarnation or religion in this chapter as to our divine purpose as this can spark a whole new angle. The problem here is that many couples do not share the same religious viewpoint. Like a friend of mine who knows a NG Kerk (An extremely "rigid" Afrikaans church) pastor with a wife that embraces the Muslim culture, although she is not one herself.

Let's get back to our chapters title, 'the concubine theory'. In our western European culture it is unacceptable to have more than one wife, but in the same culture we suffer incredibly high divorce statistics. Society has a charming way to justify these statistics by writing them down to the world we live in, work environments, high demands from our careers, stress, etc..

Now every century's inhabitants claim that they've never had life so stressful. I understand from this that in 200 years or so our future generations will look back to the year 2005 and wish they had life as easy as us. So what's their excuse going to be? To busy with inter-planet travel, having to deal with robots handling their jobs. Perhaps one of the main faults lie in with the expectations from Western civilization and our 'one man, one wife' rule?

If we look at the African Cultures for starters we observe that many have several wives. The word divorce is rarely uttered, unless they're giggling about us? From an outside observation I think these reasons keep their families stronger. There is less stress on the wives who are trying to raise children while their husbands dodge the frustrations of the Western male.

We have to honest here and acknowledge that boys and girls have very different needs and when we throw them into one home as a pair there's bound to be conflict when certain requirements aren't met. One of the two often has a stronger character and ends up intimidating the other.

This is often done unintentionally, but the end result still rears its ugly head eventually when the weaker of the two runs out of energy trying to keep the other happy.

In my case, I don't really enjoy more than 10minutes of TV, on occasion perhaps a movie while my wife spends each (and every bluddy day) watching hours of entertainments re-enacting real life which we spend experiencing each day – so where is the escape? If I don't watch TV I'm 'ignoring' her, and if I do I'm unhappy. So perhaps a balance could be achieved?

Like many other men I speak to, their wives require materialistic things. This is acceptable, but the manner in which many approach this is unpleasant. It appears to me that a large percentage of the female population assume their mates to possess a mental telepathy that allows them to know exactly what their wives want.

In their defense many men assume that their duties cease when they come home from work, and they can relax, put up their feet, and have a beer. While doing this their wife still cooks, might do washing, bath junior, etc.. This means the wife's day ends a lot later than the husbands. This is also not cool.

Let's face it, both girls and boys have been known to screw up in various situations – criticizing them is not going to help, although understanding them might offer a glimmer of light.

The problem arises when they take the 'silent stance' that is normally combined with a temporary celibacy experience. This results in a frustrated male, glares, and eventually explodes in an argument.

In a multi wife situation, there is possibly more income generated? It also allows the woman to share their load while leaving the man to focus on his level of expertise – supplying and supporting the family.

A revelation I've encountered is the amount of 'happily' married men that have girlfriends (mistresses), not to mention that many of those women are married making them equally guilty of adultery. In fact a couple we know rather well often go camping together, enjoy each others company while the one's wife is having an affair with the other's husband, which so far has remained a successful secret for many years. This frees her to do her 'marital duties' as she calls it in the bed with her husband with less stress. But you won't believe the guilt that has built up from this relationship that she has shared with my wife.

I'm sure this tale raises many moral issues regarding faithfulness. But here is an angle that my wife explained to me that actually changed my opinion. By having an affair this woman (who is actually a wonderful person, and no, I'm not the lucky secret other half!) has found refuge in some-one who she need not tolerate every day, this escape allows her to cope with the conventional acceptable method of marriage with the knowledge that she can confide in some-one that does not make the same demands as her husband – who is also a fantastic person. So it's a trade off, guilt for escape, or is it escape for guilt? – Weird!

I've found that many successfully married people enjoy a relationship with another mate who has also not found their daily presence a labor. It's also only after I've mentioned my frustrations of married life to these people that I was horrified to find out that I was one of the few that only had one partner! Wow, I hate being so slow! (Kidding)

So it seems that many of us actually practice a multiple spouse practice in secret – this should be wonderful news to Ricki Late and Jerry Springer. Imagine if they had more people coming forward, they could open their own TV station, let alone a program!

I do realize that many people might find it hard to accept the past few pages of truth, but the more I pry, the more I see we're almost living in a huge 'soapy'. So maybe it's time I went out and found myself some one to share with too, or maybe I have, mmm, the plot thickens…

Maybe when we look at the amount of hours we're exposed to in our most accepted form of entertainment, the TV, we also think that it's okay for an affair? See the chapter on the television.

Concubines might even be a better option than wives? In fact the very main enforcer of 'one man, one wife' – the Church, has many documented records in the bible where God blessed those with many wives and concubines. How many did Solomon have? I also notice that the word 'divorce' is extremely rare in the bible.

I'd really like to know at what point in time God changed our relationship conditions? Or maybe this is another man-imposed tradition as part of a conspiracy plot by keeping many too busy with their own struggles to worry about the world bullies, I mean leaders?

Look at the fruits of any rule before you condone or condemn it. Some churches priests practice celibacy; the fruits are high statistics of choirboy molestations. Had these frustrated leaders been encouraged to fulfill their biological design and purpose the stats might be greatly reduced – Woo Hoo, go Catholic Church! Hey, the dude dresses as a lady in a dress, but we call him father! Who ever wrote mankind's rules must be quite confused by now. It's also no wonder why we have so many denominations!

Remember that we all really want pretty much the same thing – happiness. We also need to know that if we are not happy it is extremely difficult to make those around us happy. So in a round about way a hidden concubine who keeps us happy will in turn help us to be happy around those we first chose. Now imagine if concubines were deemed okay? There'd be no guilt involved as we would be taught, or programmed, that this is the way life was meant to be.

Shouldn't we 'legalize' this and give concubines an acceptable role in our lives and society? God was okay with this before, so what happened?

Think along these lines. If concubines can save marriage, prostitution will decline, and many more people might just lead a happier life? Not to mentions cut down the 'aids' epidemic that threatens our existence as well as so many other STD's. Maybe society has "concubines for hire" already for the past few thousand years? We call them prostitutes!

We just debated about prostitution, this the bible (and most other religions) frown upon, while several wives and concubines were accepted in the past. Are prostitutes not to a large degree used by frustrated men? Yes, we all know that some of us are simply horny, but each of us is an individual and our hormones are quite real and have been proven to affect our thought. Read section on the human machine.

By allowing several wives and concubines I believe we might have a more balanced, happier world. Woman won't have the constant demand from men as they will share the load, and men will be able to have more purpose and possibly feel more important. (Isn't this the main reason why so many men seek a mistress eventually?)

Secondly a concubine will possibly care more for their partner, unlike the professional one! So the concubine is a friend, sex partner and psychologist all wrapped into one. Her deeds are not career focused. While the whore? Well she wants your bucks, and in return you get a fake smile and maybe even a disease thrown in for no extra charge, which might just shorten your life!

Aids has become a major threat to our 'cheating' society. Is it not possible that reverting back to the lifestyle debated here might result in less divorces, although committed to several partners, actually have less relationships over the longer time frame?

Time line comments:
Well I still think a concubine or multi wife situation could be a workable solution. As long as all involved accepts this I don't see the problem.

But I'm sure it'll be a cold day in hell before Western society and the churches will okay this. If people are happy they might just find no need for lawyers and churches? Ever notice that many (not all) in churches are looking for some form of HOPE, as their lives are not quite what they'd hoped for? Similarly the amount of divorce cases would render many lawyers without a career, what a sad twist of fate could occur. Happy people might also be keener to question the powers in control, as they will not be battling trying to cope with day-to-day living?

As for the African culture, I didn't hear about Jacob Zuma's wives wanting to divorce him? Check into South African politics regarding the skepticism of our past 2nd in charge minister and the apparent rape charge. This reeks of cover-up, not even 1% of the EDUCATED people I've spoken with believe his innocence, so our judicial system obviously knows some thing we don't?

Either way, the Zulu culture of J. Zuma allows his multi-spouse situation, and I'm lead to believe the lads still married and considering a career in politics again. I wonder what happened to his other case regarding accepting "illegal" monies. I also wonder how much these trials cost the taxpayer?

CHAPTER 11: CHOOSING THE RIGHT PARTNER

Here is a topic I think many people would not like admitting failure to, making a bad choice when emotions kick in, but regrettably it does happen. Imagine if there was a formula to ensure selecting your ideal mate, you could make a million! Perhaps there are a few and you might find them hidden in this book. It all depends on your interpretation of the chapters.

Maybe a brief read at marriage humor might lend us some insight how to find our soul mate? Isn't it strange that almost ALL marriage and relationship humor is negative, while it prompts a positive response – laughter!

Marriage humour.

You have two choices in life: You can stay single and be miserable, or get married and wish you were dead.

At a cocktail party, one woman said to another, "Aren't you wearing your wedding ring on the wrong finger?" "Yes, I am. I married the wrong man."

A lady inserted an ad in the classifieds: "Husband Wanted". Next day she received a hundred letters. They all said the same thing: "You can have mine."

When a woman steals your husband, there is no better revenge than to let her keep him.

A woman is incomplete until she is married. Then she is finished.

A little boy asked his father, "Daddy, how much does it cost to get married?"

Father replied, "I don't know son, I'm still paying."

A young son asked, "Is it true Dad, that in some parts of Africa a man doesn't know his wife until he marries her? "Dad replied, "That happens in every country, son."

Then there was a woman who said, "I never knew what real happiness was until I got married, and by then, it was too late."

Marriage is the triumph of imagination over intelligence.

If you want your spouse to listen and pay strict attention to every word you say -- talk in your sleep.

Just think, if it weren't for marriage, men would go through life thinking they had no faults at all.

First guy says, "My wife's an angel!" Second guy remarks, "You're lucky, mine's still alive."

Well the above humor tends to dampen the mood for marriage, and might not be the best jokes for the "best man" at a wedding! But there must be some truth that led to the fabrication of the statements. I'd even venture that some readers would nod in agreement with some of the statements! So how do we avoid selecting the wrong mate?

When males think with the lower brain we get a scary reality check when the main brain is able to take control again, normally during the 9-month period, the nymph to nun crossover period. Here we come face to face with the person we chose and we need to know the following: Do we have hobbies, can we talk, can we share? – God knows can we even co-exist!!

I guess the old school way of thinking of "no sex before marriage" had a lot of logic; it forced us to learn about the person before we had any crucial reason for commitment!

Some interesting trivia: In the nymph stage my wife and I made love 8 times in one day once, now it's a miracle if we get so far in a year – isolated case? No! While sharing with males I found to my horror that I was not alone – although this was also a relief that the fault was not necessarily mine.

A friend of mine once said "Marriage is like getting a new car, you like what have, but when you see your friends, well you want one of those too" Isn't human nature wonderful, most of us would like the best, so we trade in old items such as TV's, cars, Hi-fi's, lounge suites for a new one when the opportunity arises.

The problem is when in our human frame of mind we get tired or bored of our partners – these are human beings that also decided to live with us, not just a one way relationship like we have with TV's, cars, etc. So it's going to hurt everyone should time find we made lousy, or rather "enlightened" choice.

Now woman are can be equally as shallow as us bi-brained males. They often use sex to secure a healthy, but more than often wealthy partner. *(See how many celebs of 50plus marry a 20year old bimbo? Like it's a REAL surprise when they divorce later and score a home, car and huge amount of cash in settlement!)*

Here's a quick one from the internet:

Women Are Smarter Than Men
Due to inherit a fortune when his sickly, widower father died, Charles decided he needed a woman to enjoy it with. Going to a singles' bar, he spotted a woman whose beauty took his breath away. "I'm just an ordinary man," he said, walking up to her, "but in just a week or two, my father will die and I will inherit 20 million dollars." The woman went home with Charles, and the next day she became his stepmother!

Do many women marry someone who can offer security for them to spawn and produce a legacy while attending to their own primal biological programming of having to have children? I'm not saying it is a conscious decision that women make, I'm suggesting we all follow some or other primal drive within us.

You can't help but compare the human to a computer – only less predictable and I'd still rather choose Bill Gates' Windows – it least Microsoft tries to improve on its faults. As with the human race, no-one even really knows where our programmer/creator is! *(Although many religious factions claim this divine knowledge)* I wonder if the computers 'byte' of info isn't similar to the humans 'hormone'?

Some chapters of this book were partly sparked off and reinforced later to me as a result of finding that many woman do use sex to help lure their mate in. The more men I speak with as well as my own two personal experiences lead me to believe that both sexes have hidden agendas, even if they might be quite unintentional, we're simply following our biological programs. (Please ladies, let me have your angle on this – I'm sure that many males use woman for sex too, or an extension of the male ego!)

I'm equally sure there are people out there that are having the most sincere wonderful lives together, I envy them and wish them the sincerest best and hope I can also attain this one-day. But reality determines that generalizing is as risking as a survey. Reality has also proven that too many marriages fail when the nymph to nun transition kicks in. Sad, but true. One accurate survey proved that every divorce began with a marriage! (Yes, this is a bit tongue in cheek)

So all I'm trying to say is if you're not married – don't rush! Take your time. Everything has a pro and con side to it. Even celibacy, hey – you can't get aids from your hand, or create an innocent child that is doomed to live in a one parent environment should pregnancy occur and the relationship fail. Why should ANY child loose the right to a mother AND father combination due to a lustful, selfish decision just to get laid? Use a condom dammit, if it's that urgent!

I must just highlight again that although this is written from my experience, that of a male, and I might seem to blame females for the procreating hormone, this is not the case. A friend of ours has shared on several occasions that he wants a family and that a certain woman he knows is an ideal candidate for the job, she was young, fertile, pretty, healthy – now does this sound like choosing a partner or an item?

Choosing a human or a commodity?
It is certainly interesting that our friend was prepared to go ahead at this at one time while he could seriously have run the risk of messing up this persons life in the long run. Not to mention his own hurt. Luckily for both of them he decided to fold the relationship, which took a lot of courage. I wonder how many of both sexes in a parallel situation failed to make a similar decision, and now seek refuge in divorce? Well done to his courage, it wasn't easy!

The comfort zone:
So let's sum this up, both men and woman often decide to pair up for difference reasons. When the physical is greater than the intellectual we have a problem. The physical eventually dies off and then we have to get to know our partner. The only problem is that there's often a third party present – a child who had no choice in his/her arrival on this planet. They deserve the best chance of understanding this path of life by having both mom and dad loving them and teaching them – as a team. It's difficult to have a team when members are no longer in the same camp!

Marrying for a family:
Don't do this; it's not fair on yourself or your partner who will more than likely think you marrying because you have found you "soul mate!"

Marrying the one you're with instead of waiting for the right person:
Human nature is also such that failure comes in many disguises. One fear of failure is that we think we might end up alone, so rather hold on to our partner to avoid failure in the relationship department, we

fear we might not meet some one else again – you will, if you can do it once, you can do it again!

Lack of commitment:
Another reason is that you and your partner not stay together as a result of lack of trying hard enough. The difficult part is when strong emotions from one side try and hope the other will change and love us as much as we love them – this is not going to happen people! You cannot force some one to love you, remember love and like are not the same, but I'm sure they are often confused.

So how do we choose the right partner? Here is some advice:

1) Think with your head and heart.

2) Combinations of love, logic and lust all have to be met. So if one of them fail, you still have 2 to rebuild on, or at least fall back on to help. If you only had one or two combinations there's bound to be disaster should the reason to your pairing start collapsing.

3) Don't rush any relationship; your life depends on it!

On the three L's:
Love:
That warm fuzzy, cute feeling when you meet your partner to be. This eventually must evolve into a special caring and a need to make this person happy. There must be some sort of internal drive from both of you that prioritizes the other person above oneself. But, the feeling must be two way, without this you've both got problems

Logic:
This is the planning, side, thinking about culture differences, age, hobbies, religious views, and more. Where do you want to be in society? Do you want children? The logic topic could evolve into a few chapters. But we do need to connect on an intellectual level too for a relationship to thrive.

Lust:
Both boys and girls have this, and when one closes off due to Nymph gland failure, the other some times looks for it elsewhere. Even if they don't, there is bound to be a certain level of discontentment with one spouse if the other is withholding their biological physical needs.

There are other variables that we'll discuss during later chapters, such as cosmetic appeal when selecting the correct partner. But don't you still find it interesting that we seldom see attractive people marrying ugly people unless there's a material gain? Perhaps we should add the 4th 'L', we could call it "Looks!"

Chapter 12: Are We Programmable?

I never thought of this angle until my friend pointed out a startling truth that reinforces my machine theory. This morning after sharing my approach to the human way of thinking my friend asked me "What was Hitler's strongest quality?" (Yes I'm talking about the mad German dwarf that tried to exercise genocide) His answer was "He could talk well, he managed to motivate an entire nation to attempt to kill off another."

This means that Hitler was able to program others to follow mindlessly into battle with their own life at stake with speech, delivering motivational messages. He rallied a small country to attack the continent – doesn't that sound bizarre? It's like me in my collapsing car trying to beat a Ferrari! But he got it right to get the nation to try and do this, the result? Well who came second in the war? . Or more importantly, who really won? Both lost families, loved ones, homes, businesses..

Then my friend asked another bomber "How did Napoleon get a nation to walk across, I mean march across, to attack Russia in the middle of winter – it was damn cold folks, and fucking unpleasant and seems like a really stupid idea! (The lads couldn't even relax during the journey!) Yet he pulled this off at the cost again of how many lives? It seems people look up to good speakers and are known at times to follow blindly.

Now these two fellows must have had the most amazing programming skills to be able to over-ride our instincts to not want kill our own species. To confirm this, if any of these soldiers might have met each other in another situation they probably would have had an ale and laughed together. Perhaps some might even become family through marriage across country borders?

Now nothing is more prone to disaster than a badly designed program. The earliest windows users will confirm this! When someone without programming skills attempts to write something we have looming problems and severe repercussions. We must then accept that we all have different skills or talents.

I know I'll never represent South Africa as a Springbok rugby player! Similarly Jean DeVilliers (South African rugby player that came to me for a few guitar lessons – and yes, he did exhibit large musical potential for those who are curious.) might never play guitar like Eric Clapton? But can you imagine Eric Clapton in a rugby scrum? Our "heavenly" programmer certainly didn't give us all the same characteristics and strengths. So are we all equal? The key is to realize that although we're not equal, or rather do not share the same talents; this does not make us better or lesser than others. Imagine saying a musician is better that a rugby player? – *Read later chapters.*

So let's look at the average marriage. After marriage and the drive to procreate the male and female both have to attempt to provide the best for their new arrival, something that is NOT taught at school. (Go South Africa; if Thabo and his cronies get their way we can learn to say "are you hungry?" in 11 official languages" – cool don't you think? Where are the skills to provide for food and other basic skills?)

I do not for a second think that the average human is not driven with good intention. (Hey, Hitler really just wanted a better future for the German nation with his rather controversial method – which was WRONG!) And no, I'm not implying that the average human is that radical either – all the radicals seem to drift into parliament, no matter what country?

Now in a marriage we're still faced with the reality that we have two adult humans who more than likely might not agree with all the methods of child raising in a typical family situation, then we have our parents also wanting to add their wisdom. This in turn forces or confuses loyalties between spouse and parents. This means we're bound to try and convince the other our method is best – this is a form of programming.

So we get back to the nymph to nun topic. It's so unfair to expect the nymph gland to excel when the machine, or human that's housing it, is responding to an inadequate programmer. Once more we're back to basics – no one wants to be around some one we do not agree with or have conflict with. So some thing as intimate as sex is really not going to happen when we're disagreeing.

It's no wonder why woman turn from nymph to nun in nine months. We cannot blame them for their own biological changes as they change from breeder to caregiver. Yes I know it sounds crude, but in basics this is how we humans have managed to sustain our existence.

The problem here is how do we determine who the bad programmer is, as well as who is trying to program who. I think we try and do the same to each other at the same time. Unless one of the parties is incredibly stronger than the other, sort of like a Hitler programmer, there is a no win situation.

I personally think that on average women might be better programmed for the role of caregiver. Although this approach backfired on me – see the chapter titled wife number one - but has redeemed itself with wife number two.

Some where in our programming is the "ego" virus, this virus leads us to believe we can comment on the others decisions with authority, as we simply know better. Although sometimes this might be necessary, how do we know when to intervene on each other's programming?

I'd sincerely like comment on this from our medical experts, as well as from social workers. Perhaps social workers are the human equal to computer analysts?

Lesson here is:
Both boys and girls are generally pretty much okay – if they weren't, they wouldn't make the decision to team up in the first place. We, boys and girls, are so filled with stupid facts like "which famous author died in 1645" or " what is the chemical symbol on the periodical table for Platinum" while we have no idea how to handle relationships, children, etc.. Go educational system!

No wonder relationships fail so often, also what is the divorce ratio between couples with children to couples without children? Are we adequately equipped with how to manage a family? Most divorced couples I know have a legacy that now looks up to them for a divided leadership!

My question here is: "Is school simply a great idea managed wrong, or the result of the previously mentioned conspiracy theory to prevent happy relationships and contentment in the human species. Thus we never get around to confront the bullies who run the planet?"

Hey, maybe we're just faulty failing programs trying to correct our own programs and those of others at the same time without having all the variables or rather "all the truths" available to us? Perhaps humans simply cannot multi-task as well as we'd like to believe we can?

At least religion offers a great escape for our blunders – the devil made me do it!

CHAPTER 13: LOVE – THE MACHINES HANDICAP

We cannot but help think that the human uniqueness lies in our ability to love. We all search for this and find it in many places, like our partner, our children, our friends, our pets, Gods, and some even turn to material things – the love of money, or your car, etc. Perhaps we should try and explain what love is first?

Now I love my child. When I see him smile I feel beyond happy and content, when he laughs or accomplishes something that used to be a challenge I feel a sense of purpose fulfilled. I also love my wife, with not quite the same intensity, but nevertheless her happiness is important to me, I care that about her well-being and her enjoying her visit on our earth. It's also important to me that she feels some form of purpose too.

Now the opposite of love is hate, a feeling of contempt that many of us often reserve for a large amount of our countries leaders, as well as a desire to kill all rapists, and those who hurt others for their own entertainment. Yep, I would not hesitate or have any moral problem with emptying a fully loaded gun into Bin Laden or some sick bastard that raped a 3 yr old child!

Isn't it interesting that the words "content" and "contempt" sound so similar, some one with a speech problem might get these two quite confused leading the listener to be rather lost for words. These two feelings are a direct result to the situation I'm confronted with, so is it okay to assume that outside factors control my acceptance of them and how I respond to them?

GOOD NEWS FRED, YOU'RE NOT IMPOTENT, YOUR PRICK IS SIMPLY SCARED TO DEATH!

This picture is to illustrate my next point regarding love at first sight. Face it people, would you really want to spawn with the creature on the right? You'd probably be considered ill, unwell, perverted, and/or fetish orientated if the answer was "yes". Please notice there is no mention in the cartoon that she might the most wonderful person.

To date the machine does not have this desire, and the big question is – will the machine ever achieve this? Before we look at the machine I'd like to discuss some more instances of love, for example "Love at first sight".

When last did some one fall "head over heals" with an ugly person? When did your friend say they saw a grossly over weight, slouching person with grubby hair, crater like skin condition and knew this was their future partner! Did ANYONE ever lay claim of "love at first sight" on such a creature?

Look at the previous cartoon and be honest. NO! I'm tempted to say that in every case (yes 100% of the time) the target of your new found emotion had some or other pleasing physical attribute. So what was the person actually reacting to?

The answer is really quite simple, they "fell in love" with a being, who, if they were lucky enough to meet, would eventually became a person with a name and a personality. The object became some-one! This validates that our initial assessment to this "love" was purely physical.

We "recognized" love which is meant to be spiritual, and a mystical God given gift, as a result of what we saw, not who we met. If there was a spiritual connection I feel confident you'd also some times hear good looking people laying claim to this wonderful experience when they're exposed to really cosmetically challenged person from a distance.

Face it, how many "pretty" people marry the ugly? And when this occurs there's often money, status or both packaged along with the ugly one! Please note that I'm not suggesting ugly people are not nice to be with, they might even be better partners in some instances and even make better lovers than some of our sexy counterparts.

With all this said I feel almost confident that our programming, here I go again, is such that "pretty people, or rather "not ugly" people, are far more acceptable as partners, or donors for the act of procreation. We subconsciously associate good looks with a level of health, sort of a quality check for our source or recipient of sperm.

So our hormones respond better to thought of procreating with an "acceptable" partner and thus help us make our decision to "fall in love". Falling in love could then be the bodies way of telling the brain all is well, the ultimate confirmation – that's why we seek love so much. (Just a thought)

This I guess could be parallel to a form of quality control as exercised in a factory creating a certain item. The machine has parameters that test the item being made to see if it meets certain requirements, if not the machine discards the item as faulty.

The human is not much different, we look at the potential mate and see if it falls within our own personal parameters, these requirements often have strict limitations regarding health, age, intelligence, cosmetic appeal and financial independence – so where is love now? If they fail the test, of which the first is arguably the cosmetic, the other characteristics are not even open for debate. Remember, we call it "love at first SIGHT", not love at first conversation!

Now the possibility of a relationship with a person who does not meet these requirements is simply discarded and the next "candidate" on the conveyer belt of life is tested. There is a certain element of health, fitness and well being attached to beautiful people!

Now a machine might pass an item right up until the last test before it fails it, the humans are quite the same; we just take much longer to run all the tests. For example, once our first test, the cosmetic evaluation, is passed we go to the next step – yes, the potential mate to be is pleasing to look at. We use dating as our next sequence to learn about our future mate.

We then find out the age, now this topic has some very nearsighted comebacks. At 25years a partner of 40 might be very appealing, sexy, attractive, they might also pass the financial and intelligence test, so we pair up and mate. But in 10years time the 25year old is now 35, while the partner is 50years of age, so the initial cosmetic requirements are now no longer being met. Then due to the nature of our design, our requirements change, we now begin grow apart. Divorce occurs, children loose their family. Hasn't this scenario ended up on many magazines front pages?

What happened to love? I thought it was a deep, meaningful, spiritual bond – is it not once more an illusion created by certain values in a possible program that let the human machine validate it's purpose or function. Yes there are a few who do succeed, is this due to guilt or fear of the church, are they really expressing their true feelings?

If we compare human evolution to the machines, I dare to say that the machine, although not on par with us yet, is evolving at a much greater speed than us. Can we confidently say that it will not exceed us in rational philosophy later, much the same way they are already faster, stronger, more reliable, calculate more complex formulae with greater accuracy, exercise greater precision, need I say more?

Perhaps we should entertain the thought that with the right programming "it" (the machine) might become a "they" (be able to exercise all human characteristics.)

The thought for the day is, if the previous paragraph ever becomes a reality, would it be fair to not assume that we too are simply machines that are also following a program of sorts. And if so why is this such a bad thought? The more we understand about ourselves, the better we can appreciate our abilities and utilize them to the maximum. Oh yeah, this will really annoy our religious leaders as we'll know longer need them, so who's going to pay for their next car?

Similarly, the political leaders will also no longer be able to bully the populations to their own materialistic advantage. Bullies hate to be challenged!

May the love for yourself motivate a yearning to grow within and understand yourself instead of mindlessly accepting too much of the garbage that our spiritual and political leaders feed us. They love themselves enough to do this at your expense, so take control back from them!

Err, the title Mr. Author? What happened to the Nymph to Nun thing? Well here goes…

If love was truly this mystical spirit bond possessed by humans and not able to be transferred to machine, why does after all our courting, hearts in love, our incredible "MAKING LOVE", so often ground to a halt after the said nine months in question? Is it perhaps because our biological programming of procreating the species has fulfilled it's purpose, and only should the program require to continue to procreate there is no, or rather little reason for the nymph gland to work?

Is it not possible that our next experience of love might be subjective to hormones and chemical combined with a primary directive to multiply? Well if we have nothing other than this, in other words no hobbies, no interests to self entertain ourselves, and a selfish notion that our partner is responsible for our purpose and happiness, is it any wonder why divorce figures are so high?

Now please people, I'm not suggesting that love does not exist, I do not for a second doubt that loves is as real as corrupt politicians. I'm just questioning the romantic idea around it.

We, the human race, like any other animal, even the rat, are created boy and girl. We both have something the other half needs in order to sustain our presence in the universe. Our primary drive is to procreate.

Society has deemed it that the majority of the Western world works on one man, one woman relationships, sort of like one man, one vote? And our bodies are designed to experience great pleasure when attempting to reproduce, obviously to ensure we do this more than once!

Why else would I suggest that perhaps gays and lesbians are not chemically and/or hormonally balanced – I was not suggesting they're wrong or bad people, just that perhaps they're not following their biological program due to a system malfunction resulting in the body manufacturing too much or too little volumes of hormone, estrogen, etc., and that it might be corrected or rather balanced out with the appropriate medication.

Let's repeat, but in list form:

1) Boys and girls need each other biologically to maintain the human species existence.

2) We have the orgasm; a pleasurable reward for doing this deed, arguably to ensure procreation is attempted repeatedly. Perhaps

natures way of saying "Well Done, now the human species will not die"

3) To help us achieve this level of intimacy we have "love", which is sort of like saying that we're compatible on several levels, from intelligence, cosmetic, social status, financial, etc.. This ensures that we try and maintain a higher level or quality of the human in the future generations of the species.

4) Love and romance helps the pairing process to test the others creative genes, we pit our wits to win the future spouse's approval. Well so far the nymph gland is on a role and positively active. Ever notice how the dress code often differs between married woman with children, and younger single woman that are possible single – it's just their nymph gland priming them for the biological function. (When last did you see the belly button ring on a mother?) And love and romance are so much more intriguing than an application form for pairing and sex!

5) Then conception occurs, the program is fulfilled, and I think we've said enough about this. We need to find out now why predominantly males still have their small head in overdrive while the female is "complete"? Perhaps our programmer is telling us something that society does not want us to know? – Well we're back to the conspiracy theory as well as entertaining the concubine concept.

Just a last comment on the compatibility factors:
If we look at genes we might see the following odds of pairing:

1) Clever + Clever = high chance of clever off spring, although no guarantees.
2) Clever + Stupid = possibly higher ratio of average offspring – help us out here doctors?
3) Stupid + Stupid = high risk of being stupid, has the kid got a real chance?

Now I'm not suggesting stupid people create stupid children, I'm hinting that the social circles and what a child is exposed to in family life affect their power of thought. There's a phrase "you are what you eat", so what I'm saying is the outcome of many children is directly proportional to what they're exposed to. Are they motivated to think? Are their peers striving to better themselves? Does their diet allow for mental growth?

Are the previously mentioned topics not perhaps similar to programming and the design of the machine? Stronger, better-designed machines simply get the job done more efficiently.

If you think I'm being nasty, please drive past a squatter camp and hold back the tears as you view the hopelessness on so many children's faces there. No I'm sincerely not trying to be social selective. But this fact does reinforce that children are to large a reflection of what we expose them to, i.e. how we program them via standards. You'll also notice that very seldom do clever and stupid people pair up. Being stupid is not a crime, it's a tragedy.

If we are all equal, how do doctors explain the IQ point system? Why are some races better at creating new things – look what race of people the likes of Edison, Einstein, Bell and Mozart were – no one told them how to invent, no one led them by the hand, they simply had a yearning to improve while other nations continued to trade their daughters for cattle? On which continent was the wheel first made? Fact or fiction?

Oop's almost forgot about other human traits such as passion, satisfaction, greed and desire. If we think of them as different levels of motivation sort of like prioritizing things, it's not that difficult to build this into a formulae.

Let's take passion for example. This is our drive when we really enjoy doing something. Now most of us do something for a reward of sorts, it could be enjoyment, to better yourself, for financial gain, or recognition. The difference between passion and greed is the motivation for doing something and the amount of care exercised for those around you while doing it. For example greedy people will often not think about hurting some one while aiming for the prize.

Desire on the other hand might be the level of effort applied to something we wish to do, but either attempt poorly, or feel the importance of success at the topic in question doesn't justify the effort – hey, this can be a formulae too. Sort of like this in math terms:

Task + effort > reward: desire, it would be cool to do, but not really worth the while. Maybe we still do it, but very casual.

Task + effort = reward: satisfaction of the job well done, we do it for this a purpose.

Task + effort < reward: passion, here the reward for doing it, the joy, success, is such that it is great doing this, but we still consider others feeling.

Task + effort = only thing: normally coupled to greed, where we sacrifice others to attain our goal.

Now all we have to do is build in a value system that determine a point structure that helps the machine evaluate where it is with its purpose and if the result from the task is beneficial to it and we have very similar methods of reasoning as exhibited by humans. This combined with a time line concept, a few bugs and a virus for good measure, and… (Fan fair of trumpets, a loud "ta da") …we have **"The HUMAN BEING!"**

We call our reasoning for doing something, which can be sharing our life with another human, instinct and/or love. We also say we love doing some tasks. These "emotions" are often a direct result of things we've been exposed to in childhood, so once again, isn't this some form of programming?

So if a machine had the same importance level to sustain its existence and create others to take over once it expires we'd need some sort of check system to make sure the machine makes the right choices. Perhaps we could call this motivation for self-preservation "love"?

Maybe the most difficult human characteristic to build in is the ego. This and a the ability to subject itself to various viruses at random?

Chapter 14: Careers Vs Family

Perhaps we should take a step back and see our life as a progressive time line, which I believe it is. Far too often we get so involved in the present we fail to think of the future, especially when emotions and hormones get their way. Similarly we forget about what we learnt in the past. Remember folks, we cannot fight instinct.

There is a time for almost everything. Time for study, time for play, a time to meet a partner, a time for procreating, a time to provide and make your mark in life. I'd like to believe that every human has some sort of goal, or goals, although when I look at some people I can almost begin to doubt this.

For example, an acquaintance my wife and I know is as ambitionless as they come. At almost 20, their main drive is to watch TV, sleep and eat, although the sequence of events do change! For example, they can also sleep, eat, watch TV, eat, eat while watching TV, then fall asleep in front of the TV after eating, the person is talented! The fact that they would probably look like "Oros man" in an orange track suite must count against them. The sad thing is that this person is really above average intelligence with so much potential, so much to offer, a heart of gold, but with little motivation to further themself. Just so sad.

As mentioned in other chapters we can receive contentment or satisfaction in many ways. And I believe that our human nature, or rather our programming requires this so we can feel of some purpose to ourselves and to those around us. The problems sneak in when we place the responsibility of satisfaction on our partners and even friends. We expect them to keep us happy! This often happens when our career provides little or no job satisfaction.

Now before we blame our careers or rather jobs for failing us, we must realize that no one has a gun at our head forcing us to do what ever we do for a living. I was a telkom technician before I decided to become a full time musician.

After working for telkom for a few years I grew really unhappy. I used to watch the clock for home time, didn't miss a second of lunch, and even took smoke breaks to chat to my friends! (Bear in mind I don't smoke.) With my present career as a musician I've managed to diversify from teaching, to performing, developing my own plectrums, completing an instructional DVD and writing software, you'll often find me up at 5 in the morning guitar in hand! Similarly late at night instead of watching TV I'm once more planning a new software product, learning a new song or even gigging. To spend at least 12 hours working is now a pleasure!

Perhaps a career is a job we enjoy, while a job is a career we have no interest in? Listen carefully to your friends conversation around this topic next time, perhaps the most discontented people use the word "job" while the happy ones use "career"?

Now why do we stay in our jobs, why choose a lifelong labor we do not enjoy? A possible answer is fear of not getting another job? Or perhaps it's a comfort zone that you've become used to? Maybe you're a white South African male with reasonable fears of affirmative action, mmm? Then again I know some people that just enjoy bitching – that's really sad!

The saddest fact is that many of these unhappy souls now expect their partner to make them happy, to give them purpose for being here – wrong move! I once heard that only 5% of the planet actually knows what they want to do, and of that only 5% are actually doing what they want! So the chances are pretty high that your partner is looking for the same form of fulfillment that you might want, and they're turning to you to fill that void in their life. Yeah, well the wheel does turn I guess.

The lesson to be learnt here is that we must think carefully, research career options, and chat with councilors regarding options in the business place. If you're happy with how you spend 8 hours and more every Monday to Friday there's a much higher chance that you need not use your spouse as a crutch for happiness and contentment – this goes for both sexes, not just the boys! Quite often our hobbies can double as a career too – explore this avenue.

Personally I would like to blame my schooling and parents for me wasting the first 7 years of my adult years in Telkom, but the main blame I place on politicians. I choose to work for Telkom as it exempted me from military service, a requirement of our government a few years ago. I didn't see the logic in being shouted out by an idiot in a brown uniform and being brainwashed into killing people that would more than likely prefer to sit around a fire and share an ale with me.

Now if all the nations "sheep" did the same, and rather entertained our neighbors instead of mindlessly following orders to shoot at them, those arrogant obnoxious leaders of ours would have to fight their own battles.

Can you imagine George Bush, Thabo Mbeki, Saddam Hussein, or Tony Blair being shouted at and forced to climb up and down ropes? Why didn't Osama Bin Laden fly the airplane? – Because he was too scared and probably enjoys life and fears death – hypocrite that he and many other leaders are! No the buggers would rather sip cocktails in the comfort of their homes and tell you and I to do the dirty work – shame on them all! And the benefit of being a patriot to my country that I did not choose to be born in and could not afford to leave due to my passport at the time and insufficient funds was to be paid less than minimum wage, a fraction of what Telkom's wage was.

Getting back to my schooling and folks, well they just wanted me to get a job. I never once had our school councilor sit with me and chat about career options, I never once realized that I could of made a career out of sports – shame on you Mr. "high school guidance fellow".

I really think that many adults do not inform their children to what potential they can reach, yeah, I'm sure they can turn around and lay a similar blame on their parents and teachers. If we don't know any better I guess it's a fair excuse, but if we do, and simply sit on that information and knowledge it's almost a crime! Is that really the right thing to do? We can break the circle, we must stop accepting our situation if dissatisfied!

Now the real truth is NOT to blame these people mentioned above, accept they made a real bad mistake and learn from it, don't do the same! Blaming some one won't help you progress yourself, I think too many of us use this as an excuse to not do anything, in other words "Oh dear, life is so bad and it's my folks or teachers fault, I guess I'll have to accept this" – CRAP!

Others after learning this say, "What's the use, I'm too old now, or it's too late to do something about this". Science states that nature always looks for the easiest way; maybe it's easy for people to accept their fate instead of realizing they can do something about it?

Rather acknowledge that shit happened and then do some thing about it, move forward, get a life. Otherwise what are you in turn teaching your children? Do we really want them to adopt a loser's stand and accept defeat? If you're really too old to change your own situation you can still help the younger generations avoid similar pitfalls.

So what on earth does this have to do with nymph to nun? Quite a lot really! People are often attracted to people who succeed in life, we can be part of this circle too, and we can also achieve independence, satisfaction and a level of self worth if we choose to do this. Leading by example is far stronger and motivational than trying to push someone, show them what can be done, don't tell them, show them!

I'm sure people prefer sharing their success. Try and have sex with some one who cannot make you and themselves happy and vice versa? It's not going to happen easily. But let both parties be confident in themselves and enjoy their partner, not expecting them to make us happy and see if your sex life doesn't improve. When I'm happy it's a lot easier to make my wife happy.

Think about it from this angle. We meet some one, fall in love; often in today's society we also often indulge in amazing premarital sex while not living together. So we're still not in a situation where we see the other being down, we do not see them pissed off with their job. They can focus on their time alone with us and enjoy each other as an escape = great relationship and sex.

When single, a date can be seen as an escape from our mundane job and possible lifestyle. But when the target of our affections becomes part of our daily routine through marriage, we often see them as another problem to deal with, not that wonderful escape we so used to look forward to.

For those who hold pre-marital sex as a taboo, especially older generations – look at old photos and see how many of these buggers are smiling? Yeah, go to a museum, or even your old schools "hall of fame", the trend to smile often only manifests itself in more recent years. Is it safe to assume that smiles and contentment are go "hand in glove"?

So what does an emotionless serious photo tell its viewer? If you do enjoy this new almost sociably accepted pastime, just be careful for "bi-products" folks. (To the idiots, wear a condom for fear of 1+1=3. The possibility of a bi-product such as a child or a disease is a reality) – now let's return to careers!

Later we marry, live together and suddenly our escape becomes a burden. We find ourselves in a situation where we do not get a chance to be depressed about our situations by ourselves. So what happens, our escape turns into chains. We now have the extra burden of our partner expecting us to make them happy which shouldn't be the main focus, our depression brings them down, and the sex drive dies out too. The price we often pay when we blame our spouse for not making us happy.

Ever had this conversation with your spouse? "Hi honey, how was your day?" The answer is "Lousy, Joe was late, the bluddy PC crashed again, and boss obviously had a bad night, also no thanks for my last project, and no sign of that raise either" – what a great way to start a romantic evening. But imagine your spouse said this "Amazing day, I began a new project that I can really be creative in it, the potential rewards are incredible" – wouldn't you rather be around some one with this answer?

Other bi-products of unhappy jobs are affairs. This is not a surprise as we're all creatures of habit to a large extent. For example, we're married for a few years and miss the escape dating offered, and we really don't like our job. So we look for a new escape! The office affair can offer many "positive" options. We've now returned to a form of dating! And as an added bonus we look forward to going to work!

We escape our original partner to go to work to see the new loved one, while we look to our new loved one to escape from the reality of work – interesting scenario to say the least. The only down side is? Your spouse must NOT find out, so guilt becomes the call of the day!

The value of career satisfaction can greatly motivate the nymph glands drive, assuming the owner of the nymph gland is equally enjoying their career, and not doing a "job".

So ultimately it's both girls and boys that are equally responsible for the situation they're in. Yeah I'm sure there are isolated cases, but I think this is a fair generalization comment of the society we're in today, especially the Western one.

Now for the family part.
We must lead our children, I believe it's their right to have parents that show them how it's done, not dictate. If mom and dad are happy this in turn will create a healthy environment for our spawn. They have hope; they can see that the crap on TV is often fiction and that they can in turn actually find happiness in themselves. We can then guide them with what we've learnt and hopefully greatly increase their enjoyment while walking this planet.

To summarize:

1) Almost anything is possible, but we must first accept this belief.

2) We must not expect our partner to make us happy, charity starts at home, look to yourself first.

3) Blaming someone might be great in a car accident for insurance purposes, but for career moves rather learn from the failure of others, even try and help them!

4) If you don't like your job, get a career. There's no one forcing you to stay. Keep in mind your boss/employer is trying to create wealth for his own family. He never forced you to work for him, so don't blame him for your unhappiness!

5) Our children deserve to be shown hope, and options to enjoy life.

6) A family can be the ultimate blessing, provided we make the most of the situation, we owe it to ourselves as well as those around us, and have no right to place that responsibility on some one else. Striving for happiness begins with you.

Time line comments:

After reading this I still feel exactly the same way. Even more so! I believe we must encourage our children to enjoy a career. Give them hope for the future, not dwell on yesterday. Time does not have a reverse facility and we cannot bring the dead back, or even rewind our own lives a year or several. Although we're all going to join our predecessors eventually where-ever that place might be.

But all we know is the present and we can only speculate and hope our belief in what ever after life is correct. So enjoy the now, this is one certainty we are experiencing.

Yesterday is gone – learn from it.
Today is here – enjoy it.
Tomorrow is to a certain extend unpredictable – hope and prepare on it

Some fruits of keeping a despised job manifested in South Africa a few weeks ago. Our private security company employees were unhappy about their salaries, so they went on strike. Instead of being thankful for someone actually creating work for them, they opted to complain. Instead of learning from their employers and perhaps saying "Screw you, I'm resigning and starting my own company" they went the easy route. Complain, strike and expect the bosses to be "happy" to see them when they got their way.

Arguably starting their own company would have entailed an effort, but doesn't anything worthwhile require this? Didn't their lack of motivation lead them to take rather pillage Cape Town shops – assuming you saw the loss experienced by shop owners in Cape Towns CBD. The TV news scenes were horrifying.

The final outcome? They didn't quite get raise what they expected, the bosses are really miffed, and the employees still have no real control over their future! These people are living examples of those who would rather lay blame at others for failure than taking their future into their own hands.

Did they ever stop to think along these lines?

1) What would I have done with my life if my employer had not started the company I work for?

2) If my boss got it right to start a company, why don't I learn from his example and do the same? They're the proof it can be done.

3) The owner of the business never came to my door and forced me to work for them. It was my own free will to do so, as it is my own free will to resign.

A friend of mine proved that a different approach could get better results. She was unhappy with her job and applied for a new career. Upon handing in her resignation, her boss asked her what caused her to want to leave. She explained her salary was not adequate and she felt her ability was not recognized. Her boss then gave her a +25% increase, and a promotion! Everyone was happy and the entire negotiation took an hour in a civilized fashion.

The lesson here is to take responsibility! Forcing someone against their will rarely has a positive outcome.

Chapter 15: The Humor In This

Although most chapters have a cartoon and/or a joke or two, I've decided to dedicate a section of the book to forget about some of the more serious topics that are being discussed. I hope they bring out the lighter side of relationships.

What is both interesting and sad is that many of these jokes are based on actual frustrations that might have led some to the divorce court!

I equally hope you enjoy these short 'studies'. They're my interpretation of the jokes that have been emailed to me from both sexes, not just the chauvinist half. Although some scenes might not need accompaniment of a comment that relates to a personal and similar situation that has occurred?

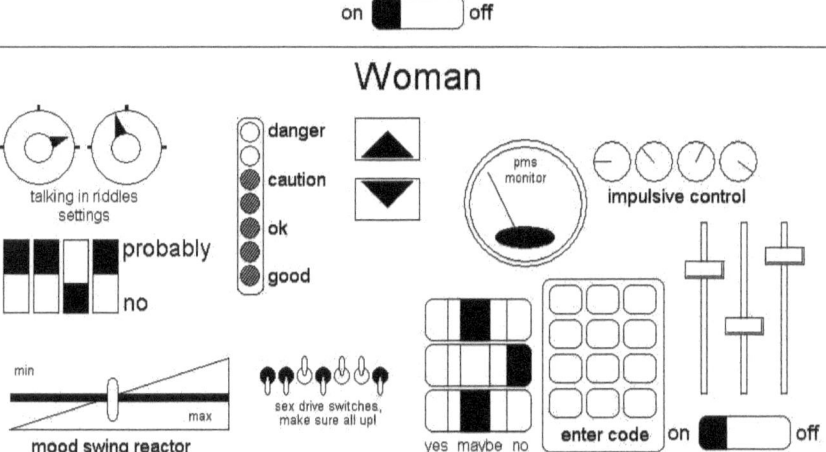

Our first diagram could be viewed as retro control panel with the top half the men, the bottom the women. Most men are thought of as "yes or no" creatures, on or off types. Yet we are sometimes 'deep', intellectual, sensitive, emotional, philosophical, etc. But it seems that both men and women agree that the above picture sums up the generalization of both sexes rather well.

The only down side is that when married the wife thinks she can control the males switch. When it 'gets stuck' well, there's nothing really left to say. Although this debate can be from either side! I just don't understand my wife's controls.

The engineer's interpretation – this email bought a lot of smiles from both my wife and I. It really doesn't require much to comments on. If any one out there has the male's specification sheet, please mail it to me.

Element : Woman
Symbol : ♀
Discoverer : Adam
Atomic mass : Accepted as 55kg, but known to vary from 40kg to 250kg

Physical properties
1: Body surface normally covered with film of paint and/or powder
2: Boils at absolutely nothing, freezes also for no apparent reason.
3: Found in various grades ranging from virgin material to common ore.

Chemical properties :
1: Reacts well to gold, sivler, and all precious stones.
2: Explodes spontaneolusy without reason or warning.
3: The most powerful money reducing aget know to man.

Common use :
1: Highly ornimental, especially in sports car.
2: Can greatly aid relaxation and pleasure.
3: Also known as very effective cleaning agent.

Hazards :
1: Turns green when placed alongsied a superior specimen.
2: Possession of more than one is possible, but must never make eye contact.

Now I'm sure that at some grey time in our lives we've decided to go shopping with our spouses, and it was probably either met with one or more of the following:

1) An argument.

2) Mild or aggravated tolerance.

3) Some one being rushed.

4) One party spending a considerably larger portion of the time focused on their needs, while the other is expected to act as wallet or credit card holder and complimentary critic. There are times when a little lie can go a long way, so please avoid 'that skirt makes you look a little plump' at all costs!

The below picture sums up a typical encounter that most males seem to endure when shopping. I'd also like to point out that any resistance from the male to this situation will only encourage the 'nun' hormone that inherently becomes less and less dormant as your partner becomes a wife and then mother. Bye, bye nymph…

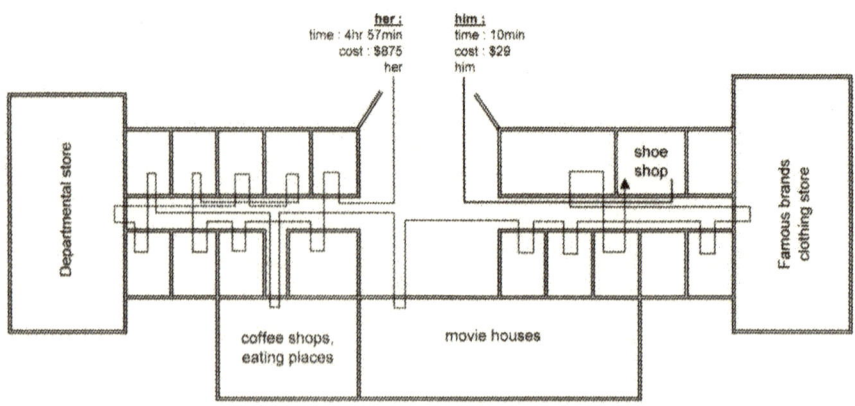

Goal : to purchase a pair of shoes

Yeah, this one has also featured before, but I also felt it needed a repeat viewing. I read somewhere that sex is good for one, but much better for two ! With this in mind my heart goes out to the poor lad in the picture below. We cannot but help wonder if he's just recently divorced, or looking for an affair. If the latter, maybe he's been married with children for a few years and this is all he knows? Either way it still bought a smile to my face.

Now in the defences of the wanker, here are the reasons why masturbating is really not that bad:

1) No chance of 'not now dear, I have a headache'.
2) You're making love with someone you like.
3) You can change hands without getting the other hand jealous. And you can wear leather gloves too.
4) No chance of Aids, or other STD diseases.
5) You can imagine who ever you like, even call their name without fear of reprisal!
6) If single still, no chance of pregnancy.

7) You're not open for emotional blackmail later, or 'do you still love me?' scenarios.
8) You don't need a condom.
9) On a medical serious note, after your eminent 'release', the hormonal balance is returned to normal. This reduces stress levels and helps the owner of the said hormones to return to normal and focus on other aspects of life such as career, hobby, etc.

This actually goes for both sexes I've been told.

Now here is one for the evolutionists. Although I'm not sure on the amphibious versus mammal complications insinuated here.

Now if you subscribe to the concept on the previous page you stand less chance of this ever becoming a reality.

Now I wouldn't recommend this extreme. But, hey – at least he's getting laid tonight? And, no! This is not a real newspaper extract, although I've read stranger things and topics like "Politician tells the truth' in the news – now who really believes that?

Eager wanker spikes own drink.

Cape Town, Saturday evening. A man who enjoys masturbating so much has admitted that he drugs himself with Rohypnol so that he may have his way with himself!

He went on further to tell the police he intentionally set out to victimise himself, he did this by deliberately spiking his wine with this sedative when he was not looking. He's initial plan was to take advantage of himself while he's defences were down.

Police have described Fred as one of the many local predatory masturbators that are presently circulating in the Cape Town area. One police Captain said the following "In fact it's tempting to say that Cape Town bars are often full of wankers.'

When I received this one I tormented my spouse with several 'woo hoo's' it got a welcomed giggle and some smiles. Once more we can understand why people have written books like the 'Men are from Mars, Woman are from Venus'. It's really sad we seem to forget to respect each other's ways and what is important to them. The fact that we are created so differently but seem to need each other so much suggests to me that our creator must have a really unusual sense of humour. Even a daily mundane task such as cleaning ourselves can spark off an argument, or disrespect for each other ways. Let's study the ritual of showering.

HOW TO SHOWER LIKE A WOMAN

*Take off clothes and place them sectioned in the laundry
    basket according to lights and darks.
Walk to bathroom wearing long dressing gown.
If you see husband along the way, cover up any exposed areas.
Look at your womanly physique in the mirror - make
    mental note to do more sit-ups/leg-lifts etc.
Get in the shower.
Use face cloth, arm cloth, leg cloth, long loofah,
    wide loofah and pumice stone.
Wash your hair once with cucumber and sage
    shampoo with 43 added vitamins.
Wash your hair again to make sure it is clean.
Condition your hair with conditioner enhanced
    with grapefruit and mint.
Wash your face with crushed apricot facial
    scrub for 10 minutes until red.
Wash entire rest of body with ginger nut and jaffa cake body wash.
Rinse conditioner off hair.
Shave armpits and legs.
Turn off shower.
Squeegee off all wet surfaces in shower.
Spray mould spots with tile cleaner.
Get out of shower.
Dry with towel the size of a small country.
Wrap hair in a super absorbent towel.
Return to bedroom wearing long dressing gown
    and the hand towel on head.
If you see your husband along the way, cover up any exposed areas.*

HOW TO SHOWER LIKE A MAN

*Take off clothes while sitting on the edge of the
    bed and leave in a pile on the floor.*
Walk naked to the bathroom.
*If you see your wife along the way, shake willy at
    her making the "woo-woo" sound.*
*Look at your manly physique in the mirror. Admire
    the size of your willy and scratch your bum.*
Get in the shower.
Wash your face. Wash your armpits.
Blow your nose in your hands and let the water rinse it off.
Fart and laugh at how loud it sounds in the shower.
Spend majority of time washing privates and surrounding area.
Wash your bum, leaving those coarse bum hairs stuck on the soap.
Wash your hair. Make a Shampoo Mohawk.
Wee.
Rinse off and get out of shower. Partially dry off.
*Fail to notice water on floor because curtain was
    hanging out of bath the whole time.*
Admire willy size in mirror again.
Leave shower curtain open, wet mat on floor, light and fan on.
*If you pass wife, pull off towel, shake willy at her
    and make the "woo-woo" sound again.*
Throw wet towel on bed.

Well, okay, I guess some of the manly rituals aren't that great, I mean butt hair on the soap is a bit much. Although the routine showering seems a lot less serious and much more fun. If only we laughed with each other more often.

The next is a valuable lesson for any man, there are ways to get around this predicament, like suggesting that your idea was actually your wife's, and how clever she is for thinking of it. So we boys have to be a bit humble here, but at least we get the desired results.

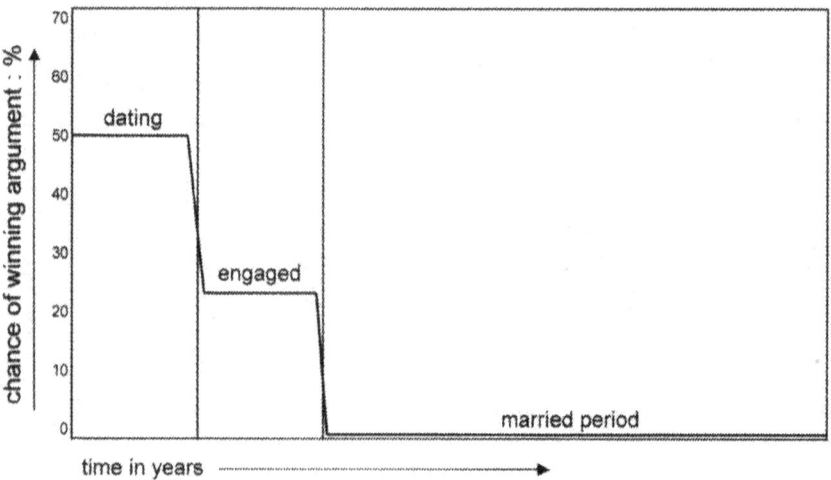

Figure 1

Even the animal kingdom suffers!
Before the marriage:

During the marriage:

And…. Wait for this….

After the divorce!

Alcohol has also started many doomed relationships. I've even heard some saying that they would never of flirted with a certain object of their animal lusts had they been sober! Something like this below?

I guess I've mentioned masturbating a few times, but when trying to please yourself, DO NOT TRY THIS AT HOME!

CHAPTER 16: PETS

This is a personal topic that almost caused wife number two and I to go separate ways. I love cats, she idolizes dogs. Now before we go further, this is not so much as cat and dogfight, but rather of priority for your spouses needs. (Please note my change in the time line later through this chapter)

But first, a quick laugh from a dog's perspective! Another email.

Who's the boss?

1. *Blaming your farts on me... not funny... not funny at all!!!*

2. *Yelling at me for barking. I'M A FRIGGIN' DOG, YOU IDIOT!*

3. *Taking me for a walk, then not letting me check stuff out. Exactly whose walk is this anyway?*

4. *Any trick that involves balancing food on my nose... stop it!*

5. *Any haircut that involves bows or ribbons. Now you know why we chew your stuff up when you're not home.*

6. *The sleight of hand, fake, fetch and throw. You fooled a dog! Woo Hoo what a proud moment for the top of the food chain.*

7. *Taking me to the vet for "the big snip", then acting surprised when I freak out every time we go back!*

8. *Getting upset when I sniff the crotches of your guests. Sorry, but I haven't quite mastered that handshake thing yet.*

9. *Dog sweaters. Hello? Haven't you noticed the fur?*

10. *How you act disgusted when I lick myself. Look, we both know the truth, you're just jealous.*

Now lay off me on some of these thing's, we both know who's boss here!!! You don't see me picking up your poop do you?

Now let's return to the serious side.

Here is why I dislike having **our** dogs around:
1) They are big dogs living inside.
2) They have NO training, and do as they please.
3) They frequently steal food, even from our child with no recourse on their deeds.
4) Their hair is all over the place.
5) The garden stinks like dog poo!
6) They bark at every thing when my wife is home, even when no one is there, but slept while my car was burgled in our driveway.
7) My wife frequently reminds me that the dogs were here before me and therefore they enjoy the right to do as they please.
8) When our child was in toddler phase the dogs often bumped him over and hurt him.
9) Whenever I eat I'm faced with 2 pairs of eyes begging, if I say some thing then I'm the bad one.
10) They are consistently under our feet and we fall over them.

Well you can imagine how these topics have certainly dampened many opportunities for the nymph gland to recover! It's come to a point that I've realized that I must make a decision. Keep quiet about these animals. (Or rather "anal moles" - you ever notice how a dog likes burying it's nose up another dogs butt?) Or run the risk of our child losing his family.

When I was a kid I actually liked dogs, after my present encounter all that has been severely tainted. (*Wait for the time line.*)

Once more this is not necessarily an attack on dogs, this can be applied to any animal. An acquaintance of ours is fanatical about birds. The entrance to the house can be described as a human aviary. Bird poo and feather line the house and their one offspring has expressed their frustration in this and surrender to me regarding the living environment that they've been exposed to.

Another friend a few years ago took to aquariums, the family car was parked outside while the garage was lined with fish tanks, enough to challenge most pet shops I've seen! The financial expense of this impacted the family, and I really don't think I need to go on further.

The lesson in this chapter is balance, as well a sense of understanding if your children or spouse do not enjoy your fanaticism as much as you. My aunt for example breeds budgies of international competition standard. But the birds live in a dedicated place outside the house and do not intrude on her children or her husband's home.

The result being that every one is happy; my aunt has her hobby, which does reap substantial financial rewards. My uncle also enjoys the birds as he doesn't have to live with them, the children are happy as they have their space and their mom and dad is happy. You see, it can be done.

What I'm proud of is that my aunt and uncle have actually showed us that it is possible to do a hobby to it's full potential without effecting the family. They've also demonstrated that hobbies can generate income. To them I say "thank you".

The difficult part is what to do when your spouse holds the rights of the pet in question higher than that of their spouse? Or rather expects you to understand their love for them and demands you share this view "Shame dear, they're only animals." You have no idea how good it made me feel when my wife repeatedly pointed out that the dogs were here before me!

I had to shut down and accept this or else live in constant fight over the animals. The pending result in my case would more than likely have been a split at our child's expense. My present wife is quite a complex life form, the most stubborn and compassionate at the same time, depending on the topic in question.

What we need to realize is the impact of selfishness regarding animals. If you hold resentment to your spouse due to an uncomfortable living environment, are there not bound to be less of a drive for forms of intimacy?

Similarly, the perpetrator of the fanaticism is more than likely to sense your discontentment, so now we have both partners not really motivated, so the nymph gland is bound to stay dormant, no matter which sex is responsible.

Well, now the time line kicks in!

About 5 months ago I bought my wife a Labrador/Ridgeback cross. All went well for the weekend, but with me working from home the puppy took to me as his bestest friend. (This is not a spelling mistake; you have to meet Cosmo to appreciate the childlike attitude.) Needless to say the fast growing tornado of love and destruction is now a 30kg monster with a wagging whip of a tail, terminal itching teeth and a distorted belief he's a mole! Well he's my dog now and I wouldn't swap him for the world.

So let's look at how my opinions have changed:

1) I still wish they would be living outside, they are huge dogs. But luckily our child is quite older and can stand his ground should the dog's be a nuisance. I still think it was wrong to have exposed him to them when he was still a toddler as mentioned before though. I would still like them to have kennels for when the family needs a bit of space, but I've learnt to live with it, and actually sincerely enjoy the 12 black legs on patrol in our house.

2) Now I have 3 pairs of eyes when I eat, but at least my wife now helps me keep them at bay – sort of a give and take attitude on this level has taken place between us. Although hopefully not too late?

3) I'm now also allowed to reprimand or help quiet barking sprees.

4) Hairs – well, we try to ignore this, sort of mutual sacrifice.

5) Under our feet still? Wow, it's like a black tidal wave down the passage when these 3 dark beasts follow us down to the kitchen anticipating food or a handout. But I've learnt to live with this too, even seen the funny side of trying to 'surf' 3 dogs while dodging from one room to another?

Well the new addition has helped me understand a lot about my wife regarding her attitude towards dogs, and even though I don't agree with all of her methods, we're certainly getting along a LOT better on this topic. And I apologize for being too rigid here before.

No one said it would be easy to understand the others reasoning when not viewing it from the same angle.

Chapter 17: A Religious Stance

This is a delicate topic and I'd hate to offend anyone. My goal is not to sway some one from their faith, I believe anything that gives hope and makes us a better person without hurting or compromising others should be encouraged. Perhaps I should first explain my beliefs and opinions to help you understand my angle.

I am presently not a Christian, although I do believe there must be a creator. Neither do I subscribe to any other religion, eastern or otherwise. I would also like to point out that I do not claim to have 'the truth'; neither do I believe anyone else to have the complete truth. There seems to be flaws in all religions, which is not surprising as we're all human.

SERVICE CANCELLED

SO THE PRIEST IS UPSET WITH HIS 10% AND DEMANDS 8% EXTRA !

Some history as to my religious background:

I used to be a committee member of my school scripture union group and later was also confirmed in three churches while searching for the truth, I am a member of the Methodist, Anglican and Vineyard churches. I have "given' my heart to Christ, and have decided to embrace the scripture "those who seek the truth will find it" – see comments on this later.

During my first marriage we studied with Jehovah's Witnesses, Mormons, and tried several other "conventional" Christian churches to try and get God's purpose in our marriage. Regrettably nothing happened as wife number 1 insisted we move from one religion to the next as soon as her thoughts or values were questioned.

Here are some of my beliefs, theories and observations before I go on to the nymph to nun topic. It can be viewed as my personal creed.

1) I believe that all religions must have something plausible otherwise it could not exist or be sustained.

2) No religion has the absolute truth; if it did we all would follow it.

3) All religions are unfortunately abused by some of its members, usually one of its teachers or guru's that turned greedy or began to revere themselves as a God.

4) History is full of documented facts how people killed each other, stole, pillaged, raped, maimed, and conquered in the name of one God or another. Too many people have been killed as a result of religion for me to embrace one.

5) Perhaps man cannot deal with the fact of death or dying one day and he creates religions to believe that he will live forever. Personally I do not fear death any more. If I am dead and I do not know it as I no longer exist, why and how can this be a problem? If there is an afterlife and a judging God/creator then I rely on that God/creator to judge me on my sincerity to

my beliefs based on my limited understanding. As well as my attitude to others.

6) With so many people 'passed on' you would think at least one of the millions would of given us some reliable, un-speculated, undisputable insight into what happens when we die.

7) I think it's sad that so many religious leaders threaten their followers with a "hell" of sorts if the follower fails to obey the faith in question. And then also makes promises that they have not at any point been validated to make. These religious leaders are no better than most politicians – shame on them, and on mankind for being so gullible. I believe the scriptures to write, "who ever seek the truth will find it", and at no point does it provide any clues or hints as to when we might have found this truth!

8) My limited physics knowledge does lead me to believe that there is a creator, the big bang theory and evolution just has too many loopholes. My high school science taught me something cannot come from nothing. As for an evolutionary approach, I doubt if my future generations will suddenly begin to grow wings if we need to fly? If evolution was true, why did some creatures fail to 'climb out the ocean'? Surely if all life forms started at the same time we'd be at the same place of evolutionary development? (Unless we're actually NOT equal!) And didn't Darwin himself admit to several flaws in his own theory and retract a lot of his beliefs? Come on people, if the 'mysterious ape/man' existed, there'd be one helluva more skeletons found, not so many faked findings – speak to an educated Jehovah Witness that knows his research on this. Or just think about it for yourself. Its real difficult for me to swallow this theory "Millions of primates, then a handful of "cross over man/apes" and lastly millions of humans. It's basic math people, not rocket science!

9) I also find it difficult to accept that a God created us to worship himself! *(Where do our gifts to God end up? After a pittance feeds the poor, the pastor buys a new car, home, jewelry – ever seen the Vatican's riches, or Ray McCauley's new Mercedes? - Stop being so gullible!)* Now to return to an almighty creator. It's like having

141

children so they can praise us. Isn't this a strong insecurity complex? I think it sad that anyone creates something to tell him (or her) how great they are, although a creator of this magnitude deserves credit, do you really think he/she really needs praise from a faulty species?

Well that's my 'creed' if you like, let's get back to the title topic. We were created man and woman, each with a purpose to procreate the species. Science tells us that we, like the dolphin, enjoy sex.
Well I know that I enjoy sex and I didn't need science to tell me that. The hint of nice breasts and other various woman attributes and I get a very pleasurable feeling inside that is quite removed from procreating – I just want to get laid!! Not to mentions all the benefits from a healthy sex life.

Please, I'm not just a horny person, I do actually love to make love to my wife too, even thought this has reduced in her 'nun' phase of life. I also do love her as the wonderful person she is, not just for the potential physical satisfaction I might get from her.

Our doctors have listed these reasons as why sex is good for you

1) Sex is a beauty treatment. Scientific tests find that when woman make love they produce amounts of the hormone estrogen, which makes hair shine and skin smooth.

2) Gentle, relaxed lovemaking reduces your chances of suffering dermatitis, skin rashes and blemishes. The sweat produced cleanses the pores and makes your skin glow.

3) Lovemaking can burn off those calories you piled on during that romantic dinner.

4) Sex is one of the safest sports. It stretches and tones up just about every muscle in the body. It's more enjoyable than swimming 20 laps, and you don't need special sneakers!

5) Sex is an instant cure for mild depression. It releases endorphins into the bloodstream, producing a sense of well being and leaving you with a feeling of well being.

6) The more sex you have, the more you will be offered. The sexually active body gives off greater quantities of chemicals called pheromones. These subtle sex perfumes drive the opposite sex crazy.

7) Sex is the safest tranquilizer in the world. It is 10 times more effective than valium.

8) Kissing each day will keep the dentist away. Kissing encourages saliva to wash food from the teeth and lowers the level of the acid that causes decay. Preventing plaque build up.

9) Sex relieves headaches. A lovemaking session can release the tension that restricts blood vessels to the brain.

10) A lot of lovemaking can unblock a stuffy nose. Sex is a natural antihistamine. It can help combat asthma and hay fever.

(This is an extract from one of the emails I received, from a woman friend I might add, I hope she's practicing what she preaches?)

It certainly seems as if sex is a good thing for both men and woman to enjoy. It also seems to me that our creator made sex for us for many reasons other than just procreation.

Doctors lead me to believe our body needs all the bi-products such as endorphins, antihistamines, etc.. And in turn a healthy sex life can help ensure a healthy mind and body. If this is how we were designed by our creator, why do so many people fight this? And is it fair to say that married woman with children that change from lover to mother suffer the most from a hormonal swing that causes them to ignore their own bodies needs as well as that of their partners – please ladies, doctors and professionals – your comments are welcomed and will feature in the next edition of this book.

How many divorces occur before a child is born?

143

Arguably most divorces leave a child crying for both parents. How can we get to the best possible solution without fair and accurate information from both sexes, hey, maybe men are simply just horny mammals, or perhaps my assumptions are not as general as I thought them to be.

I believe that statistics have also proven that statistics are often inaccurate. To validate this take a survey of who likes Britney Spears at an Ozzy Osbourne concert. The result could possibly reflect that 99% of the people asked dislike her. So when a survey is taken, I wonder just how often certain groups of people are targeted to be questioned to produce the required stats, another example is that less than 5% of my friends have faith in our government – but they're still in power?

During the last election I was at a garage when the attendant said to me "those bluddy kaffirs in parliament". The interesting thing is the he was an African! So if a petrol attendant doesn't believe in our government (the ANC), how did they get into power? The plot thickens.

Let's get back to religion. Has any one ever seen a God? The excuse of "He's to great to be seen" is simply unacceptable. The loophole in this statement is that if God is so great surely he can make himself visible and still create an impression on us lowly mortals. I think it's our leaders keeping God at bay so they can manipulate us to follow their doctrines on His behalf.

As a loving father I really enjoy spending time with my child, he knows I'm there, he doesn't have some one else stand in for me, he has the real thing – his dad. He can hold my hand, see me and talk to me - what's my heavenly father's excuse?

Now for those who might say they've seen an angel or heard God talk to them. Were you mentally stable, sober or drug free? No I'm not being sarcastic, but any of the just mentioned three could induce illusions that seem quite real. ("Reality is an illusion caused by the lack of alcohol." a friend of mine once said with a perverted smile on his face.)

Wouldn't the one true God guide his creation rather than leave them to blunder their way through life guided by perverted, greedy leaders? How do we know when it's our own thoughts or God's voice we hear? Faith can often lead us to put our deranged actions on Gods shoulders! For example, "God said I must kill them!" So faith does have a certain level of convenience for unusual actions.

Mankind wrote the bible, although claimed to be divinely inspired. It's amazing how certain "books" in the bible were left out to help validate a certain churches beliefs; similarly how certain translations vary to accommodate the sect that uses it. Please try and read the book about the Da Vinci code regarding this. And now we learn that the scheming Judas Iscariot was actually Jesus' best friend?

For those that are not aware, it was on national TV that we viewed a documentary where the book that Judas wrote was unearthed and translated with some unusual turn in events. That Judas and Jesus agreed regarding his purpose in history, and Jesus trusted Judas as his best friend to help him with this divine sacrifice. I wonder two things:

1) Is this the truth?
2) If so, how many truths are still to be found that conflict with ancient teachings?

Lets have a look at some dubious Christian teachings:

The trinity:
A Christian favorite is the trinity theory. The more traditional churches, Catholic, Methodist, Anglican, Vineyard for example, believe in a trinity, a sort of three in one Godhead. The father, Son and Holy Ghost. Nowhere in original scripture does the word trinity or its counterpart exist!

But if look into history there was a time when pagans and Christians tried to "compromise", one of the Christians churches contributions were to accept a "3 in one God" belief, just to keep the pagans happy. What, you didn't know the 3-in-1-god idea was derived from pagan belief?

Is Jesus God, or his son – further trinity conflicts?
Original scripture if translated correctly claims, "The word was A God" not "The word was God". Keep in mind that Christ is referred to as "the word" in some denominations. Now even if the correct translation is not correct, why does the scripture fail to mention the missing third entity – the Holy Ghost, or Spirit? Isn't it also interesting that God is talking through so many Christian denominations, but the lack of continuity is such that we have too many variations? Remember the Irish's Anglican vs Protestants scenario? Some one is misquoting God folks, and your leaders claim this privilege.

When something is done in someone spirit, it does NOT mean a new mystical being has manifested itself as a 3rd party!

Christmas day:
I suppose you didn't know that the 25 December was one of the most important celebrations of the pagans too – now it's Christ's birthday? Just look at the fruits of Christmas, the highest death figures, the highest amount of drunkards out and about, most financially viable time for material things and business. Yeah, you may call me Scrooge if it makes you happy, but look at the facts people.

So when is Christ's birthday?
As we just mentioned the Christmas debate. Christmas, which was one of the pagan's biggest holiday/festivals/calibrations is meant to celebrate Gods sons birthday, and God wasn't originally very keen on Pagans if I recall correctly? Now suddenly the Christians claim our Christ was born on the 25 December – WRONG, by several months, no-one seems to know the exact date, but we have proven it to be quite a few months out! I also don't recall **any** place in the bible requesting us to make Christ's birthday a celebration either.

The fruits of Christianity
My old scripture union leader, as well as many pastors, have taught me we can judge a person or event by the fruits it bears. If we look at the fruits of Christmas, today's most revered religious holiday, the death toll alone should scare the crap out of you! Then there's the amount of

alcohol consumed resulting in infidelity, fighting, hangovers, and this is all in the name of God folks – He must be really proud of us! Doesn't the bible teach that we should make decisions based on the fruits of the belief? *(Oh yeah, isn't it interesting that Santa is actually an anagram of Satan?)*

Many religions claim that their God is our father. Now I'm a dad too. I know the following:

1) Let some one try and hurt or rape my child – I'll kill them if I'm aware it's happening. Why does our heavenly father sit back and allow this? This goes for ALL religions, not just Christians.

2) I did not have children to tell me how wonderful I am. I tell them how wonderful they are! I am not that insecure to rely on praise from my child to give me self worth.

3) If we are created in God's image then we might assume this. "If we are dumb, then God must be dumb, and a little ugly on the side". Now this quote is not my words but that of Frank Zappa, a famous musician from the 60's to the 90's. Try and argue that God is perfect but his creation flawed and you have the theory of being created in His image seriously in jeopardy. How can we be a reflection of God and at the same time be nothing like him?

4) There is no way in hell that I'll send my child to his doom by flying a Boeing into a building, taking many innocent lives! So where is Bin Laden's divine source coming from?

Should there ever be an advert for "God wanted", I'd not apply for the job. *(Any way, I think most political leaders are fighting for the position.)* Imagine being represented by men who often want power and material value, or the job themselves.

You have to love our Bishop Tutu in South Africa. The lad has written a book of his own prayers! Now I was taught that pray is a **personal private** time when we talk to God. So why are we so dumb as to want to open our wallets to read Tutu's prayers? Who benefits from the fruits of this deed – why Tutu's bond account people!

Where is the privacy and sincerity in feeling that the prayers of others work better if they PURCHASED! Are we so insecure with our relationships in our God that we need to ensure financial gain for the likes of Tutu who is arguably more politically involved than most in cabinet? Lastly, doesn't the bible tell us NOT to combine politics and religion?

So let's stand back and review this from another standpoint. Tutu sells books. He makes a fortune for allowing us the privilege to read his HUMBLE words, yeah right! Now how many other ministers, pastors, priests, etc, have done the same?

Now from what I've seen is that the present God(s) don't get allowed to speak much. If they are truly speaking through our religious leaders then we have the following problem!

There are too many religious denominations claiming divine enlightenment, which means either God has a serious split personality, or there are several Gods, or only one of the thousands of religions or denominations actually really are telling the truth. So we have this situation now:

1) There are actually several Gods. This is the only way to justify or rather accept the words of our all our various spiritual leaders.

2) Assuming there is only one God – who is actually representing him or her accurately. In 1914 both Germany and England lay claim to the same God as their troupes were blessed before battle. Now on our little blue planet we have so many more divisions called denominations, sects or even cults that I don't have enough fingers and toes to count them. Remember, if there are 100 people claiming Gods word, at least 99% must be wrong!

3) Let's say all the religious leaders are hearing the same God. We now have a seriously multi-personality, twisted creator turning his own people against themselves and intentionally dividing nations and destroying relationships due to religious beliefs. That, or our

listeners need to have their ears cleaned! This doesn't sound very much like a loving fair God, what do you think?

At the end of the day we might assume this, "God only knows, and he's not talking". Quote from David Lee Roth, one of music's best front men and vocalists.

Here is my prayer "Dear Creator, should I be completely off the mark while trying to understand your will, please forgive me as this theory is my honest sincere attempt to understand who you are, or if you exist. Perhaps one day I might come closer to absolute truth and still be able to correct any of my statements listed in this book. If for no other reason than just trying to understand why everything is."

The above prayer is NOT tongue in cheek! If God is whom the Christians perceive him to be I humbly ask His forgiveness and the opportunity to learn, I am seeking truth – the bible demands this of me. (Keep in mind that each belief has some truths as we discussed earlier.)

Similarly, should the Muslims or any other religions be right I ask the same enlightenment. I'm not trying to condemn any religion, my "attacks" are rather focused on those who have twisted and perverted the most wonderful ideals for their own gain. May there be a hell set aside just for them!

May we all learn the truth eventually? Even if it means we must die first.

Time line comments:
Well my dad has passed away late last year, I've not yet heard from him although I talk to him as if he were here and listening to me asking him for some sign, but just silence.

On his death bed the military minister came to 'bless' him an hour or two before he passed on. It was really sad, this dude (the minister) seemed as if he was going through a rehearsed prayer with little sincerity. He asked the typical clichéd questions of my dad who could barely understand or even acknowledge our presence, let alone focus on praying for his soul though all the drugs keeping cancers pain at bay! On completion of his "job" (the minister again) he wished us all well and went on his way waiting for Friday, or was it pay day?

What still haunts me was my dads illusions, he saw the painting moving above his bed. He also couldn't follow conversation and repeated himself; the machine was failing and dying.

With the picture, it wasn't the frame, but the waterfall was actually running he claimed. He also looked really scared the last hour, but maybe it was also the pain, or perhaps confusion, or an angel coming to help him? He had cancer and his pain thresholds were tested continually. At least I got to say goodbye and tell him I loved him. But the uselessness I experienced by not being able to help, or even communicate with him was soul destroying.

I'm still not in favor any religion for myself, I still hope to find God, the truth, or what ever it is that's out there responsible for our existence. Maybe my dad now knows?

Chapter 18: Is TV Really On Our Side?

This is a very personal topic to me; I really feel that society has a lot to blame for it's own condition. Let's take a typical day for many families.

1) Wake up about 6:30 – switch TV on to see news, weather report, and cartoon to entertain children.

2) Work from 8:30 until 5:00, come home, cook, clean ourselves, watch TV for escape. And is the TV great for the children? It annoys me how many parents see the TV as 'something to do' for children instead of playing with them and getting in quality time.

3) Go to sleep after last TV show of interest.

4) For new couples, even have sex before sleeping – I can still fondly (or was it fondling?) remember those days…

5) On weekends wake up when hangover allows or guilt of letting TV entertain children kicks in. Do shopping, clean house (not necessarily in that order) braai (sort of like a barbecue), watch sport – yep, you guessed it, on the TV! Wash, shower or bath, watch the movie, which is surprisingly on TV! What ever happened to drive-ins where the whole family went out? Did the movies get too expensive or does TV make us to lazy?

Although I'd like to swap the husband and wife around in the above picture, I'm sure that both sexes might feel the above situation possibly relevant to their situation.

Now what gets me the most is what society deems as okay to watch and the result of all the negative input from this flickering screen. (Yes I know there's also plasma screens too, but you know what I'm getting at)

TV topics

1) **Soapies** – here somebody is screwing somebody else's wife while they are being sued by an epileptic lawyer who was actually the twin brother of the husband from the previous marriage to a nun who led a double life as a prostitute to make up for the priest who molested her hamster as a child! Who says this

garbage has to make sense? Now many say it's an escape, my problem is – an escape to what?

2) **Legal shows** – here we have 1000's to choose from, each has a handful of attorneys and lawyers all arguing with their personal morals and trying to lower them just enough to make their clients bank account break without compromising the firm they work for. If they do, we enjoy the intrigue of watching them trying to outwit their partners while often battling to come to terms with their confused sexual desire. Hey, when you screw so many people it's bound to confuse one of their own sexuality? Go Alley McBeal!

3) **Comedy** – more often cynical, or cheap, we seldom get anything new anymore. But at least they're trying to make us laugh. It's amazing too how we enjoy the "candid camera" shows, it really sad that we have to embarrass others to make us laugh, are we so pathetic that we need to be made feel better by watching some one else seem stupid?

4) **Reality shows** – has anyone really stopped to wonder why the contestants are so stereo typed. They all have pure white smiles, designer haircuts, speak in a similar manner. At least these shows save the studios that produce them a fortune on actors, scriptwriters, and goodness knows what else lies behind the scenes. Or maybe they aren't so spontaneous; maybe they're all following a plot after all?

5) **Music** – if I see another poor, deprived singer with nice cars, beautiful women, tons of jewelry shout at me with topics of 'how bad he has it the ghetto' I'll hurl. Let alone the lack of creativeness on how he or she would like to screw their partner. What ever happened to clever stories, play on words, etc? It seem that rap is an excuse to not write melodies, or even learn how to play an instrument. I do believe that music education is failing our children at schools. Even the 'idols series' is bordering on a farce. It more of a fashion statement, why else is there an age restriction, and only beautiful people allowed enter, or rather make it through? And before I forget, what does the

intro credits say "Idols are dressed by SomeShop" Music has become a fashion parade and if the artist can sing a bit, then we have a bonus! When I asked a friend why he likes Usher and Justin Timberlake when their lyric content is so shallow and their singing skills average he replied "But have you seen them dance?" Need I comment further!

6) **Murder and drama** – well here we have uncharted waters – NOT!! Someone has once more killed, raped, or theft of a rare government code has occurred and the earth lives in fear of pending doom! So now some genius detective with some or other weird habits or dress code, or a Ferrari driving hunk gets to solve the case. I'm not sure if this is educational instruction to help prepare criminals from getting caught by showing them how the law thinks or a form of entertainment. Either ways, violence, deceit, death is all the call of the day.

7) **Sci-fi** – Well this is a personal favorite, at least here one can escape. You have to exercise a certain level of imagination to be absorbed by the story. I've yet to date not seen an alien, a flying saucer, or heard some-one say 'beam me up Scotty', so at last I can escape into make believe. Okay, so it's not real everyday day life, we have to be a bit creative here, something too many people are losing the ability to do! Now I dare you to argue that exercise and imaginations are bad things!

8) **Horror** – Here we have the spawn if Satan on the loose, or some twisted deranged person wielding a chainsaw in a mask killing for fun. It's amazing how the human mind likes being entertained by pictures of others being killed in the most horrific way, or by stories of how we screw each other both figuratively and literally.

9) **Emotional tearjerkers** – In this exciting fast moving plot someone's soon to be late aunt has an unpronounceable disease that no doctor or religion can cure. Yeah, not even Billy Aids Virus and Billy Graham combined can help! (did I spell his name right? Maybe the name Billy is the problem?) Once more the viewer chooses to depress themselves by getting emotionally

involved in this slow moving tragedy. At the end the aunt dies, her twin sister inherits the house, that is later to be taken away by the embezzling brother who happens to be the priest who abuses hamsters! Oh yes, I forgot to mention that this will be the plot for the sequel. What ever happened to happy endings where we went away feeling good about life and have some level of faith in justice?

10) **Talk shows** – here the average person can pat himself on the back that they probably aren't like the charming intellectuals as seen in shows like Ricki Lake and Jerry Springer. It's amazing to hear my wife and my mum in law scoff and comment at the commonness of the interviewees. Even the audience mocks them and criticizes them. Is this really the height of our entertainment value, to look at idiots and ridicule them? Where is the creativity and imagination in that? Did any body ever stop to think that an invitation to take part in such a talk show spelt problems for you! When last did any one on these shows walk away happy, or still with their spouse and/or lover? Face it, if you're invited to be on Ricki's or Jerry's stage, there something drastically wrong with your life – and the world is going to be your audience - that's about to happen! But still the idiots flock to get mocked!

11) **War movies** – It's amazing how God gets quoted as blessing both sides of the battlefield – at least one of the two must be wrong? We also get programmed into how noble it is to kill or die our own species for religion, belief, greed, race, while most people would rather just sit and chat with an ale around a fire. Now who tells us that it noble? The answer is: Those that never seem to get to the front lines! This has an element of convenience. You have to admire how politicians can rally an entire nation to kill. And while we do the terminating our fearless leaders sip whiskey behind locked doors. Where's the bravery in being out of range? (Long live Roger Waters and Pink Floyd) The human species can really be a bunch of sheep at time.

12) **Porn** – the ultimate taboo! This teaches us how we can make love to our partners and enjoy each other. We also get to loose a few kilo's, keep fit, prevent stress, need I say more. Now I'm NOT for animal sex, or group orgies, gay relationships, or screwing around with anything that moves and if it doesn't, then kick it until it does. But I don't see any problems with a couple in love enjoying intimacy. We all have built in hormones and are also here as a result of sex. Maybe if it wasn't such a taboo topic there'd be less teenage pregnancies due to the inquisitive human nature and a lot less divorces as couples would enjoy this gift and not get so frustrated with the often boring sex routine. So how many positions do you know?

Let's do a quick overview of what TV encourages us to watch, and what we in turn deem sociably acceptable to be entertained by:

Murder, violence, kidnapping, rape, wars, deceit, greed, lying, cheating, - we can make this list quite longer. While watching this we are restricted to our favorite chair and a glass of wine, beer, coffee or tea. The brain is then numbed into a hostile exposure of violence, deceit, scandal – ever thought that values you're entertained by eventually alter your programming to accept them as okay? But should we happen to find a one-minute clip of two people in love doing 'what caused us all to be here' we frown upon it!

I really think that there are too many people simply accepting and absorbing the trash fed to them via satellite. What happened to games such as chess, cards games, Ludo, Monopoly – where we could sit as a family and talk to each other, where we laughed and exercised our brains to make the most out of what we were dealt or the situation we find ourselves in with the game at hand.

I also think that many couples also compare themselves to the relationships on TV, especially from a cosmetic point of view – this would justify why many feel inadequate. Our spouses aren't as sexy, our homes are not filled with designer furniture, our cars are not luxury, our clothes and jewelry are less expensive – need I really say more. At least the show "married with children" is more realistic, but then it certainly doesn't give much hope in marriage.

Maybe a little less of the tube and a more creative mind and enjoying our spouses and family could lead to nymph glands being rekindled instead of dying due to being a passive patron of the box?

But don't take my word on this, lets look at TV guide and see what they have to offer: On Monday 7th November 2005 the South African TV guide had this advertised:

Soapies : Bold and Beautiful, Generations, Days of your lives, Zone14, 7de Laan, Isidingo, All my children, Egoli, Back stage, Passions, and the Young and the restless.

Soapy Comments : Many of these appear twice on one day, so it's not like the TV company is not trying to force us to watch this crap. Now let's look at the sub title of Bold and Beautiful for this day "Stephanie wants Felicia to say what's wrong" Ooh, isn't this spell binding material? Hey I almost forgot that Ridge and Thorne can't work together anymore – what a catastrophe! Are our lives so bland that this quality of TV guide write-ups actually inspires us to watch these shows? Is your life so mundane that it seems like a good idea to escape to these parallel situations – I truly believe that too many people might need to get a life and actually DO something? Is there any creativity or imagination being sparked by being entertained by this caliber of show?

Talk shows: Oprah Winfrey show, (Also appears twice in one day – the human species needs assurance that there's people out there worse than them – it's comforting that we're so self confident?) Ricki Late, Dr. Phil

Talk show comments: No write up on these shows in this day's paper. Perhaps we all know what to expect, one of the following topics (Especially for Ricki and Jerry) Lesbian teen pregnancies – well that's a challenge from me, but more realistic, "mom sleeps with son's gay lover", or "I'm overweight and my dads secret lover won't knit me clothes!" Yes I know I'm also condescending to their level, but if you don't know the quality of participant and topics discussed by now on these shows then you never will. At least Oprah has integrity, with valid motivational topics such as surviving abuse, or conquering cancer. Thank you sincerely Oprah for trying to boost and encourage people, by lifting them and giving hope, unlike the sad counterparts that regrettably share the same show description you do. May Ricki and Jerry learn from your example. I feel the same can be said for Dr. Phil, he is also trying to build people, help them understand they can function as individuals. So at least Dr.Phil and Oprah offer hope on TV.

Legal shows: The district and Judge Judy.

Legal comments: Well this Monday was a lot quieter than Tuesday with The District (again), CSI Miami, Law & Order, and Kevin Hill. Gather around criminals and study how to avoid the law by learning the working and thinking of our greatest fictitious detectives. Cool, so who died, why did the Psycho do it, how were they killed – it comforting to see all the warm family topics that we spend time viewing being so graphically and realistically displayed on national TV, blood and all. Woo Hoo, go human race, give our children this inspirational pass time, it's no wonder crime is on the rise, do young people think it's okay if we're forced to watch it on TV?

Reality shows: Feel Good Challenge, Idols, Fear factor.

Reality comments: I'm not sure if Feel Good Challenge is a reality show and I'm to scared to see if it is. As for Fear Factor – the theme is "let's see if we can break the contestant by attacking their natural fears and exposing them to situations they would doubtfully ever experience in real life." I suppose the challenge of testing one's inner strength has its merits, especially for a healthy sum of money for the victor. But did you ever stop to wonder why 95% of the contestants are "drop dead" gorgeous? Definitely not a reflection on the population outside the studio.

I'll never forget the one show where beautiful woman were lowered into a tank of water to test how long they could hold their breath for. When lifted from the water the audience was entertained by sexy woman in wet t-shirts. Was this coincidence – NO! Simply a cheap, yet clever marketing ploy. Once more I'm fascinated that humans like to see if some one will break under stress, imagine our success stories if we focused more on building than breaking? Once more thank you Oprah and Dr.Phil.

Comedy Shows: Married to the Kelly's, Two and a half men, The Rookie, Malcolm in the middle, Madam and Eve, The odd couple, Kevin and Perry go large.

Comedy comments: 2 of our 5 chancels have no comedy this evening. Three of the comedies listed here are movies. Two of the movies are to be shown when most of the population are sleeping due to work tomorrow. What we might assume is that laughter is not the priority of those who wish to entertain us, they'd rather supply us with soapies, legal, and various other more negative content shows.

Music: Idols, (arguably more of a reality show than music?), Gospel Gold.

Music comments: As for idols, I feel sorry for the contestants; they're being psyched into thinking that they're of the same caliber as the professional they're copying. Within 3 months or so they are driven to emulate the likes of Billy Joel, Whitney Houston, etc, those that have been doing music as a passion and career for years. These superstars have been living their lives as musicians, now how on earth can we expect the same from young inexperienced kids! They're a lot younger and some might not even have existed for as long as the professionals have been performing, they also might not have entertained the thought of being a professional musician until now. When they fail, the judges get to knock them quite hard, and some times praise the most mundane attempt – so I can't but help wonder if there's just a slight chance that our panel, or the producer of Idols don't already know who is going to win! Face it, you must be young, all the contestants are model quality, none are pro singers, so where is the main market – doesn't the main intro credits start off with "contestants dressed by SomeShop". Are they're searching for singers, or representatives and models working under the guise of singers?

Murder and Drama shows: ER, and some others.

Murder and Drama comments: These often overlap detective and legal shows so please apply a similar, if not the same verdict I wrote in that section. Oops, I almost overlooked "United States of Leland" – well maybe if you write a story about a depressed teenager who kills an autistic child you can also earn 4 stars. Why do so humans prefer being entertained by tragedy? And this get aired at 8:30, so we can all watch it, even our teenage kids who are looking to the media for positive motivation. What the hell is positive about a story that focuses on killing some one – and please do not use the "we can all learn some thing" side step that is so often used today!

Sci-Fi: No aliens or space ships today.

Horror shows: I know what you did last summer,

Horror comments: Well no actual satanic demons, just a psycho on the loose, once more our dark side gets entertained as we wait for the next murder and who the deranged tormentor is! Hey, at least it's an escape I suppose.

Emotional tearjerkers: (also referred to emo's) This is also closely linked with drama. Nothing on today's viewing. These plots often have a similar plot to soapies?

War shows: Nothing either for this day – Woo Hoo again!! I suppose the powers that be have decided we've been bombed with enough negativity via soapies, drama, legal, and otherwise that they need not have to glorify the nobility of dying for your country, who made you pay for this privilege I might add! (I'm sure you pay tax in some form?)

Porn : Nothing for today either.

Porn comments: Well we prefer to see it as adult entertainment, weird I thought most adults preferred to expose themselves to violence and the above mentioned, but complain when their sex lives are poor! Sort of ironic, don't you think so? We'd rather get laid than killed, but when it comes to viewing we'd rather watch killing and condemn a good screw!

Just for curiosity I counted viewing time for the following types of entertainment during the time of 7:00 and 23:00, the times that the majority of us are awake. I'm happy to validate my comments with these figures :

	Monday	Tuesday	Wednesday	Thursday
Soapies:	11	11	11	11
Talk shows:	3.5	3.5	2.5	3.5
Legal :	1	4.5	1.5	1.5
Reality :	2	1	0	0
Comedy :	4	2	3	3.5
Music :	2.5	0	0	3
Murder, drama:	3	5	2.5	4
Sci-fi :	0	0	0	0
Horror :	0	0	0	0
Emotional :	0	0	0	0
Porn :	0	0	0	0

These stats are based on the TV guide for the dates 7 to 11 of November 2005. We in South Africa have 5 channels to choose from and the times that I selected are from 7:00 to 23:00. These hours were selected as this is when we possibly have the highest percentage of viewers during a 24hr period.

Don't you think it's rather sad the amount of times we're actually been asked to exercise our imaginations? While the majority of the time the "tube" displays negativity and failure (especially in relationships) for our entertainment.

So you might ask, why do I mention Sci-fi and Porn and other titles that have 0hrs viewing time? These do take place, but often on weekends and/or more often after midnight. My wife was horrified to find two people of the opposite sex making love at 1 in the morning, but found escape in watching people kill each other on another channel! It's no wonder her nymph gland is near death.

Similarly there are other topics, for example you can watch our genius intellectual politicians make decisions for us that won't cost them a cent. This takes place every weekday for about 3 hrs in South Africa – perhaps this is the only time they work?

There are also the **cartoons** that I feel too many adults use as a side step to avoid spending time with their children. Adults seldom enjoy cartoons, but we do benefit from them. These feature daily with over 7hours of viewing available, not as much as the soapies I might add.

As for me, I LOVE cartoons, at last I'm challenged to indulge my imagination and see the often-distorted mockeries that the creators of these cartoons mold on day-to-day life and logic. May cartoons live forever!

Then we have **info-mercials**; or rather we're bombarded with "the most amazing invention" in the world. We can solve our fitness crisis, ensure that our cars never suffer mechanical failure, train the brain to be just short of perfect (or was that better than perfect?) We can clean our homes with space technology with a touch of a button, and so much more. And all this is attainable if we simply dial "the number on the screen".

Wow! We are so lucky, for a small cost we can live in a perfect world, or damn near perfect, we can all look like models, drive forever, remember every one's name and telephone number and never, never again suffer a red wine stain!

Now the TV does have a few more topics to offer such as, educational programs, documentaries, nature shows, and actually really interesting programs too.

Interesting that some children education programs are shown when kids are at school. And those who do not or cannot send their kids to school due to financial situations cannot afford TV either. Do these programs actually reach their target audience? Or is it a convenient sidestep around our inadequate schooling system with the attitude that there are alternate forms of education?

Let me say that I do not think the idea or concept of TV is bad, it think it's just become an easy way to do nothing under the guise of "watching or being entertained" without asking ourselves if we're watching something with any merit. I say shame to the viewer who moronifies them self to accept whatever mindless crap too many of us are exposed to.

The lesson here is **"BE SELECTIVE!"** to what you use as an excuse for past time. Remember that we are not islands, we are living examples to each other whether we choose to be or not. Our children look to us for inspiration, remember they're here as a result of our needs and/or beliefs, not theirs.

"Hey, Author! What about the book title, you know the nymph to nun thing?" Well let me ask you this question. After being exposed to the above topics as discussed in this chapter, do you still find any encouragement from this wonderful box of "entertainment" to help you or your spouse actually get on your feet and help yourselves? Or do you join the 44million couch potatoes; I mean spectators and simply observe life!

(I "borrowed" the concept of being one of the 44million spectators from a bill board advert that actually had the audacity to do just that. It was regarding soccer if I recall correctly. Our great media controller invited you to become one of those who simply watch. But hey, no one is forcing you to resign away the bulk of your precious life watching the few succeeding at theirs, I guess the fewer participants, the less the challenge for those who seek greatness?)

To the men: if you feel the nun gland is running rampant in your wife, ask yourself how you can motivate the re-growth of the nymph gland. Although hormones do play a large role, there are many other avenues that can re-kindle its strength, like getting rid of negative exposure for starters. Try and find a hobby **both** of you enjoy, preferably one that involves some form of exercise, even dancing. It's no good if only one of us enjoy the hobby.

To the woman: It's no wonder that after nine months of biological trauma, hormonal changes, financial stresses, lack of sleep you need something positive in your lives to escape to, something that can encourage imagination, not remind you of your living conditions. What does your TV do for you? Try the same advice suggested to men, it can work!

We, both men and woman, rely on TV, as it's easy. I believe the TV has a HUGE social responsibility to encourage us more and not promote surrender and negativity, unless there is a conspiracy plot afoot? See the chapter on this.

But in the same breath, we have the choice to accept the drivel they feed us, if we choose otherwise they'll have to adapt to us, not the other way around. Ask yourself "how the hell did the human race manage to exist before TV?" We might get some really great inspiring answers

Lastly there are scientific facts regarding the effect a 50hz flickering screen of a TV screen has on a human's brain. Even my PC monitor has a negative effect, this is why we have protection filters for PC monitors, hey now there's a market for you – design protection filters for TV's. It's a lot cheaper than a plasma screen!

Seriously though, our minds were not designed to be exposed to long term flickering of these "tube" designs, much the same way a fluorescent tube has been directly linked to headaches.

There's so much more to the human design that I don't understand why a perfect God would design us this way and then expect us not to build these things when being blessed with a creative mind! Unless he didn't foresee us going there, this lack of insight would in turn undermine His perfection wouldn't it? Many people have been killed for this idea in the middle ages, I think the term was "heresy"? So let's hope I don't 'disappear' a month or two after publication!

Maybe God's just human after all!

Quick addition, I must include!

Woo Hoo!! It's 8:00pm on Sunday and the TV has not let me down. The movie is that of Troy. The dude from ancient Greek times as portrayed by Brad Pitt. I just stepped past after putting our child to sleep to hear this quote "We'll put the greatest Greek warriors against the other "nations"" – I forget who they were fighting again, and it's really not that important. It's amazing how easily some leaders can send people to their death for glory, although self-defense has it merits I guess. I really wish warmongers would simply "grow up" and enjoy life!

What we have here is one person who is subjecting human lives to kick the living snot out of the neighboring state. Brad had decided to send men to their death, just like the idiots who were giving him a hard time.

Is it fair to say that often thousands are killed as a result of one or two people that do not see eye to eye? The result, many die, kids lose parents, wives get raped by the winning country's men – although this is so seldom gets mentioned! Mmm, society still offers some hope and dignity and draws a line about what's really not cool by trying to hide the actual nasty truths.

Go read some real life stories about Vietnam! So once more the media tries to justify the nobility of war. Come on people, let the arrogant fight their own battles; it'll make a hilarious comedy, with possibly a better ending. Can you just imagine Saddam Hussein stalking through the bush trying to sneak an attack on George Bush who is in the shower in the middle of a battlefield. While Robert Mugabe is waiting to see who will win from a treetop, possibly eating a banana?

Or, maybe war is just another method of population control installed into our basic programming? – That's a sad thought!

Time line comments:
Nah – no change, cartoons and sci-fi are still my preference. To validate my conspiracy story, TV1 has now removed it 7:00 to 7:30 cartoon in the morning that my little boy loved to wake up to. Now they have a bunch of LOUD obnoxious teens promoting really poor quality music, screaming at each other and really not saying anything at all other than giving the impression that it's okay to be mediocre. If the artists do sing, we're often exposed to near naked babes pushing their fanny or butt

towards the camera or at least making suggestive sexual moves. And now we wonder why AIDS is spreading so fast. Duh!

Maybe I'm go buy 1000 blank tapes and record them full of cartoons for those rainy days…. Speaking of which, my favorite, invader Zim is on now – see you in half an hour.

Chapter 19: The Human Machine

The more I write the more nervous I get regarding my thoughts when I read it. Like most humans I don't deal well with rejection and the thought of being told I'm an idiot for my ideas is quite scary.

Here is quite a great email I received with a tongue in cheek 'technical support' story on our programming, it goes like this:

Dear Tech Support:

Last year I upgraded from Girlfriend 7.0 to Wife 1.0 I soon noticed that the new program began unexpected child processing that took up a lot of space and valuable resources. In addition, Wife 1.0 installed itself into all other programs and now monitors all other system activity, applications such as Poker Night 10.3, Football 5.0, Hunting and Fishing 7.5, and Racing 3.6. I can't seem to keep Wife 1.0 in the background while attempting to run my favorite applications. I'm thinking about going back to Girlfriend 7.0, but the uninstall doesn't work on Wife 1.0. Please help!

Thanks,
A troubled user.

The reply is as follows:

Dear Troubled User:

This is a very common problem that men complain about. Many people upgrade from Girlfriend 7.0 to Wife 1.0, thinking that it is just a Utilities and Entertainment program. Wife 1.0 is an

OPERATING SYSTEM and is designed by its Creator to run EVERYTHING !!! It is also impossible to delete Wife 1.0 and to return to Girlfriend 7.0. It is impossible to uninstall, or purge the program files from the system once installed. You cannot go back to Girlfriend 7.0 because Wife 1.0 is designed to not allow this.

Look in your Wife 1.0 manual under Warnings-Alimony-Child Support. I recommend that you keep Wife1.0 and work on improving the situation. I suggest installing the background application "Yes Dear" to alleviate software augmentation. The best course of action is to enter the command C:\APOLOGIZE because ultimately you will have to give the APOLOGIZE command before the system will return to normal anyway. Wife 1.0 is a great program, but it tends to be very high maintenance. Wife 1.0 comes with several support programs, such as Clean and Sweep 3.0, Cook It 1.5 and Do Bills 4.2.

However, be very careful how you use these programs . Improper use will cause the system to launch the program Nag Nag 9.5. Once this happens, the only way to improve the performance of Wife 1.0 is to purchase additional software. I recommend Flowers 2.1 and Diamonds 5.0!

WARNING!!! DO NOT, under any circumstances, install Secretary With Short Skirt 3.3. This application is not supported by Wife 1.0 and will cause irreversible damage to the operating system.

Best of luck,
Tech Support

Well that takes care of the programming side; I wish I could take credit for the genius words listed above, but no luck for me. So let's return to a more serious tone.

Nerves – the human sensors.

Let's compare the human to a mechanical device. We have a nervous system that reacts to pain much the same way a protection device on a machine might shut down that part of the machine, the entire machine or at least alert the operator to a problem. Some complex robots will retract their probe from a threatening object much the same way we would retract our arm from a fire for example. The nervous system we're lead to believe works on electricity much the same way the machine does. So far we're the same.

Pride - the stubborn drive to complete a task.
Men and machines can also be stubborn, both are known for trying to do something beyond their design until we burn out. Try and drill a hole with an electric drill with an under powered drill and you stand a good chance of burning it out, the machine breaks as it does no realize it's limits, pretty much the same way a muscle or ligament tears or breaks if under to much stress.

Like machines, humans often do not know their limitations unless the correct data has been pre-programmed into them so that they can detect when stress levels are at a maximum. In humans we blame pride as our motivation to break ourselves when refusing to admit defeat. With machines we see it as an inadequacy. Fuses are normally designed to prevent burnout. So maybe pride is the humans fuse, when it's value is to high, the human burns out!

Awareness – the human's advantage?
So we can compare the response to realization that a task is too great simply as an awareness to our limits. If we do not have the information regarding the task at hand we have no idea how challenging the task might be! Yep we're still the same. Yes, some humans ignore warning signs, but then so do faulty machines!

The brain – our unique, creative computer.
We both have some sort of controlling point, the human a brain (okay so men have a little brain too, now are you happy ladies?) while more advanced machinery use a CPU, a sort of computer that controls the machine within it's design and parameters it's designed to work within. The advantage the machine has is that does not forget its purpose as easily as it's human counterpart, neither does it try and compromise

while attempting its work. Its program is arguably more stable than ours? So some men (yes, and women) and machines have a brain of sort. I'm sure you've seen some humanoid creatures walking the roads with a blank stare, and possibly no active brain!

A quick humor filled email. Here's a method to keep your brain in prime condition, although I wouldn't recommend it!

As explained by Cliff Clavin, of Cheers. One afternoon at Cheers, Cliff Clavin was explaining the Buffalo Theory to his buddy Norm.

Here's how it went:
"Well ya see, Norm, it's like this... A herd of buffalo can only move as fast as the slowest buffalo. And when the herd is hunted, it is the slowest and weakest ones at the back that are killed first This natural selection is good for the herd as a whole, because the general speed and health of the whole group keeps improving by the regular killing of the weakest members. In much the same way, the human brain can only operate as fast as the slowest brain cells. Excessive intake of alcohol, as we know, kills brain cells. But naturally, it attacks the slowest and weakest brain cells first. In this way, regular consumption of beer eliminates the weaker brain cells, making the brain a faster and more efficient machine. That's why you always feel smarter after a few beers."

WARNING: The consumption of alcohol may make you think you are whispering when you are not

The quest to better ourselves.
Here's a quick obscure theory: If mankind designed the machine to be closer to perfection than himself and this is an evolutionary development from creator to creation, does that mean our creator ironed out all his bugs in our design?

If we are to assume we design our creations to improve on our faults, then it is an interesting concept to entertain that our creator might have made us to perfect his fault or shortcomings? This in turn might suggest that our creator could be more faulty than us? Just an outside but nevertheless logical thought. Let's go back to the topic in hand.

Mobility
Movement, yes most machinery and men can normally move, although some chose to simply observe. In fact most machines move faster, more reliably, more efficiently, more practically and for longer time durations making them more useful than a mere human!

The medical profession is now relying on robots to execute precision operations due to great accuracy than any human can. This is one example of the creation exceeding the creator.

Food and energy.
Both creations need a source of energy; this can be food and water for mankind while it's electricity and/or oil for the machine. If I recall correctly our brain impulses are also electrically controlled, this can actually be measured in milli, or is it microvolts? So we're both powered by electricity of sorts!

Illnesses and injury
Now both men and machine function really well provided certain parameters are met. When a machine breaks we call an engineer for a design fault, or a mechanic for the "moving" parts. A breakdown on the machine can be mechanical or a bug in the program. With humans we have injury or mental illness, notice the parallel?

With humans we have doctors for the moving parts and a psychiatrist for the design. The sad part is that we tread very lightly when it comes to the psychiatrist, most humans fear being regarded as dysfunctional, almost as if we would choose this? If we have flu, or sprain a muscle our friends sympathize, but if the chemicals don't balance in the head we are often avoided and deemed insane. Like you can 'catch' insanity as if it were a common cold? Duh!

Now we can replicate most the chemicals and hormones in laboratories which means we have physical, tangible items much like oil, and lubricants in a machine – you see, we're still pretty much the same still.

Emotions.
What about awareness and emotions cried the philosopher and religious fellow? Let's tackle the easier of the two first.

A few years ago, I think it was around 1965 we congratulated ourselves with the achievement of putting a man on the moon; the computer was the size of a house! Today's laptop is more powerful than that machine. So in less than 50 years the exponential improvement in technology and forms of artificial intelligence is beyond impressive!

Now we have machines that are infinitely smaller and more powerful. These machines have awareness due to their programming. While I was typing this book my PC was very kind to correct spelling and grammar for me, it was aware that I made a mistake and changed the errors as its program required.

Similarly, due to the nature and complexity of modern software we can tell the machine how it should react to a certain situation, this in turn means the machine, courtesy of it's program must have some form of awareness, an awareness that was NOT present in machines 40 years ago.

So who's to say it cannot react better to more intricate situations as the programmer (creator) learns to give it options and variable to calculate it's decision in the years to come? Once the machine is "aware" of itself and is programmed to procreate it's own as well as preserve it own existence we have science fiction arguably becoming reality!

This can also be applied to small robots, they're programmed to be aware of their surrounding and adapt to them as they experience them. Awareness and self-awareness are arguably different, but maybe that's because no programmer has been able to build this trait into them yet? Maybe self-awareness and self-preservation are the next step for our human creators to pass onto our next generation of machine. And so the movie Terminator becomes a reality?

Historical facts.
Now before you giggle too loudly, go back to the year 1200, give or take a century, and claim you could light up a room with a switch and a light bulb, you'd be asked "what is a switch?" If you spoke of cars and cell phones you'd be burnt at a stake for witchcraft! Even a hundred years ago walking on the moon was unspeakable for 99.9999% of the population, you'd be mocked for suggesting this. So am I being so far fetched?

I'm really quite convinced that advance awareness exercised by machines could quite easily surpass ours with them making much better judgment calls within most situations. The processing speed to analyze almost any predicament is far superior to that of man. I guess that's why we use calculators, why are many modern doctors using machinery for operating – because they're more stable and accurate and can relay information back to the doctors faster.

I dare say that Windows can multitask better than the most educated human with a better accuracy and reliability factor, although it was design to do so by a human, thus proving my theory that the creation can be a vast improvement of the creator. This is possibly why we prefer them to man. When they fail, it's normally the human that buggered up the command.

When they do break, well they were made by us, weren't they? This in turn proves that perfection is never attainable.

What is love, and can a machine enjoy it?
What are emotions? Things like happiness, love, fear, hatred - they're often directly linked with hormones, or chemicals. Let's assess some of these and start with happiness, a sense of well-being. This is a result of chemicals being given off or released in the brain.

Doctors have proven this. Ever notice how we can swing from happy to sad in under 2 seconds? Is this chemical control a direct result of brain programming? - This is a direct question to the doctors.

We can also be happy after using the drug E, or "ecstasy", as this controls the chemicals. So once more our programming "allows" us to be happy, and says "all is well". I realize that some people might argue this, as it removes their "humanity" from them. There's also a saying that money cannot buy happiness. I'm not convinced, give a friend some cash and watch them smile!

All I'm suggesting is that we respond to a more intricate awareness that results in chemicals inducing these "physical" emotions. There was an article on TV that stated that murderers, especially those who assassinated the famous had a much higher count of a specific chemical. If this is the case, and the chemical balance was rectified, would the assassination still taken place?

Similarly, I've heard that gays and lesbians have different levels of certain hormones, if this is the case should we not treat this as a condition? Shouldn't we offer a chemical, or drug/medicine to help? And if they acknowledge this would the chemical balance rectified by a drug/medicine revert them to a "normal sexual" preference? Hope you enjoy the next giggle?

HEY, CAN I BUM
A FAG ?

SO I ASKED HIM FOR A
CIGARETTE AND HE
BEAT THE HELL OUT OF ME!

Yeah I know I'm opening a can of worms, but when I heard voices and saw movements that weren't there I was treated by a psychiatrist as elements in my brain were malfunctioning, the medicine "fixed" this. So why is it a bad suggestion that someone who is confused about their sexual preferences might be suffering from a chemical and hormonal imbalance too?

I was clinically depressed a few months back and went to a psychiatrist after being prescribed incorrect medication from my doctor that made me even more depressed. The psychiatrist changed the medication and a few weeks later my entire outlook on life, my "emotional" levels, were corrected much the same way a machine functions better when it has the correct lubricant.

Malfunctioning machines are often slow, and are known to make noises that indicate some thing is wrong. Well I couldn't wake up easily and I also complained a lot, I made noises! After the human engineer analyzed me. Explained how certain fluids were imbalances I was "fixed up". A month later I was no longer slow, and didn't make near as many noises.

All I'm suggesting is that artificial intelligence is perhaps a possibility providing all the criteria regarding evaluating situations can be adequately programmed. I'm not the only one entertaining this thought, a lot of the sci-fi movies have been written around this theory.

If emotions are really governed by mankind and were God given, not a program, then why do so many kill, steel, cheat, seek power – I believe it's a result of a faulty program. If we were so clever, so brilliant and independent and head above all the other creations, why do we have so many faults? Hey, who knows, perhaps my program has run amok and my reality is severely distorted priming me to type all of this. Let your processing of these ideas decide if I'm a lunatic or not.

What I do know is that science is evolving faster every day. Yesterday's dreams have become today's reality. I do not have the complete truth, or even a worthy portion of it, I'm simply searching. Neither does any other mortal have the complete truth; see the section on conspiracy as well as religion. PC software is evolving at an alarming rate – who knows what might be reality in another 100 years?

If we are able to pass on all our senses, emotions (via an equivalent to hormones) and all the other human qualities then we could have an equal in a machine. If man and machine react, think, logic the same way, what is the difference other than the method of construction? Man uses meat for its body, machine uses metal.

The primary difference men and machine will be the morals exercised by the machine, the speed with which it can make a decision, the efficiency of how it performs and the percentage breakdown due to it's mechanical make-up. Perhaps the next created species is the next level of evolution?

Now how does man being a machine tie in with the nymph to nun story? Really quite simple. Humor me and assume the human hormone is like a byte of computer info.

The male byte tells the male CPU that's it has certain levels of fluid that need releasing. The human program is such that the release is coupled with procreation of our species, so we are naturally inclined to want to "get laid", the need is subconsciously quite high, a level of urgency is attached. Society has deemed or rather programmed that this is the correct way to go. If we do, the fluid levels return to normal, another byte/hormone says all is well and we can function normally again.

But, what if female recipient of the fluid produces bytes/hormones that refuse access? What if the nun gland in the female provides hormones that refuse to receive the fluid? Well the male's pressure builds up and gets frustrated, society has programmed him that masturbating is wrong – go Catholic Church. And he doesn't know how to shut down this byte.

The male now has other alternatives to consider, he has an affair if it happens too often, or he relies on prostitution. Both which could produce another life form on this world, and often gets exposed some time or other destroying the family. I'm sure this is what the Church wants?

Compare this situation to a steam engine, the pressure gauge indicates excess pressure, a valve of sorts must be opened and the pressure must be released, otherwise the container blows! A human "blowing up" could be in form of temper, depression, rape, and lack of self esteem (As society suggests that only attractive and nice people get laid.)

We MUST remember that it might be the male's natural instinct to preserve the human species; this manifests itself as a stereotype horny human. On the bigger picture he is simply doing what he needs to do. As for the woman who has done her 9month conversion, she has accomplished her goal, and now has the task of raising the result of the previous mating ritual. She is also doing what she needs to do.

We have to change our way of thinking, or adapt society to help, it's unfair for the female to feel guilty for the nun gland much the same way man shouldn't feel guilty for having this drive. Once more the lads in the bible had the concubine thing sorted!

The lesson here is that being a machine or a human is not the issue. What is important is that we realize and accept that there are chemicals and hormones inside us that affect our moods and decisions. We need to acknowledge and accept we can change the way society thinks.

Conforming is not always in the best interests of the human species, this is why change occurs. Sort of a human evolution, maybe Darwin might want to suggest the growth of a new appendage that "satisfies" the male organ when abstinence occur? Of course this might take a few million years so it doesn't help me. (Yes I am kidding)

We ALL have physical, tangible elements that we can control, these can steer us off course if not kept in check. It's our responsibility to keep these in check should we fear or even have a hunch there's a problem. We owe to ourselves as well as our partners and we definitely owe it to our children who don't know better yet.

Keep your human body well "tuned".

Chapter 20: What Do The Famous Say?

Let's take my favorite inspirational people, the musicians. I did think about actors, but these poor people spend so much time living into their characters, you're never sure if the character portrayed on the silver screen is a fair reflection of their character, or if their studied character has influenced their own life.

We'll look at some of the topics as sung about by these famous artists. Those who we draw inspiration from, those we respect, people we some times think might just have the answers to life, the universe and everything.

Cher : Do you believe in life after love?
The title of the song is either a question or a statement. If it's a question then I must answer "Yes there is", for me it validates that we must first be happy with ourselves. We too often loose so much, if not everything, when we've experiencing a failed relationship.

Kiss : Do you love me?
One of rocks most long-standing rock bands, here we have the age-old question – "do you love me, do you really, really love me?" Is it surprising that men so famous ask this question? Are the women looking for security or love when chasing after some one like this? Perhaps the Eagles verify this with "Lying eyes".

Meredith Brookes : Bitch
This song is genius; it outlines the basic programming parameters of the female human. She's a bitch, a lover, a child a mother, a sinner, a saint and she doesn't feel ashamed. None of us should be ashamed, we're simply following our biological program in a body that is subject

to irrational failure due to chemical imbalances, hormonal swings and god knows what else! So when she says, "Take me as I am", you have to admire that she's found herself and content her design. This should make this song the female national anthem, maybe even the model for males too?

Brian May : Too much love will kill you
The wisdom in this song lies in the fanaticism exercised in trying too hard to find love. I was dismayed how an acquaintance of mine thought the topic silly, she in turn was desperately looking of love, so much so that she failed to see her own life decline. She didn't seem to notice her downward spiraling emotional state and consumption of alcohol as an escape – alcohol does provide a temporary, illusional reality. Yes, sadly the search for love was killing her.

Eagles : Lying eyes
The words from these lyrics strongly lead to a concubine theory. It's a sad tale about a woman who married an elderly man, probably for wealth. She now looks for consolation in a younger partner. She lies about visiting sick friends to her husband while escaping to her hidden lover. It also seems that her husband is aware of this, "you can't hide those lying eyes" sings the Eagles. Another happy ending? Not!

Ozzy Osbourne (Black Sabbath) : Paranoid
"Finished with my woman, 'cos she wouldn't help me with my mind". So one of my best musical mentors also fell into the routine of hoping that a spouse could provide contentment. When I read more of this genius' words and compare it to what the reality TV-show depicts him as I feel and immense sense of loss. I truly believe him to be a wonderful person that has possibly become a victim of trying to live up to a conflicting image of what he thinks society expects him to be. For those who doubt this, get a copy of the album "Ozzmossis" and listen to the words in the song he wrote for his son, called "My little man".

Cranberries : Zombie
I chose this song to justify mankind's zombie like attitude to accepting the will of our wonderful heroic leaders. In the one verse the Cranberries

explain "It's the same old theme since 1916, in your head they're still fighting, with their tanks, and their bombs, and their guns." They also echo the loss of life that many men just don't seem to worry about when it's not theirs. In the first verse they say "Another head hangs lowly, child is slowly taken" You can only imagine the sense of loss experienced by the death of your child or loved one.

A friend once commented that women should run the world, at least they won't send their children to war.

Cat Stevens : Father and son

"But take your time, think a lot, think of everything you've got. For you will still be here tomorrow, but your dreams may not." Here we have a wise man, he describes how priorities change as we go through life. He also points out the value of appreciating the value of enjoying what you have, this means sometimes we need to step back to see the big picture. Being single is also not a sin and almost every scenario has a up side to it. Sometime we're so focused on what we have that we forget what we haven't. Is the grass really greener on the other side, or does your lawn need mowing?

Eric Clapton: Bad love

This man is arguably one of the world's best contributors to the music world. In this song he sings, "I've had enough, bad love. I need something I can be proud of, I've had enough. Bad love. No more bad love". Once more the search for love and fulfilment is placed in the hands of another mere mortal. Remember folks, placing happiness in something probably secures a better chance in a relationship. If we swap hobbies we stand little risk of hurting someone, but try trading your spouse in and watch the tears, sadness, anger, and generally really "bad love" responses.

Pink Floyd: Another brick in the wall

For me this band sums up life as we know it. I believe they are one of the few that actually think about what they say, have contempt for the world leaders, and content in their approach towards life. May their music never die! Just a quick question, "why do we never see them on TV anymore?" Is it due to lack of commercial value, or are those in control scared of their truths and thought provoking questions?

To summarize:
This chapter can go and evolve into its own book. The amount of songs written about failed love and relationships, as well topics on corrupt politicians, are almost infinite. Now combine these with the search for truth as to be found in the gospel sector and we find that our breed of mammal has some really disturbing issues.

We seek happiness in people or a God. Again, doesn't charity start at home? I do not believe that it is a crime to make yourself happy. Don't both divorces and splits in religions result from us misinterpreting the will of the one from whom we seek happiness from? When we fail, we seem to blame them and try and change them – and the new denomination or relationship is formed.

Seeing that many relationship failures result in tears, let's take a fun look at how to write the blues, as mailed to me by a friend.

"THE BLUES"

1. Most blues begin "woke up this morning."

2. "I got a good woman" is a bad way to begin the blues, unless you stick something nasty in the next line. "I got a good woman, with the meanest dog in town."

3. Blues are simple. After you have the first line right, repeat it. Then find something that rhymes. Something like this: "Got a good woman, with the meanest dog in town. Got a good woman, with the meanest dog in town. He got teeth like Margaret Thatcher, and he weighs about 500 pounds."

4 The blues are not about limitless choice.

5. Blues cars are Chevies, Fords and Cadillacs. Other acceptable blues transportation is a Greyhound bus or a southbound midnight train. Walkin' plays a major part in the blues lifestyle. So does fixin' to die.

5a. You cannot have the blues in a Lexus, BMW, Benz, Jaguar, Volvo or any SUV.

6. Teenagers can't sing the blues; they ain't fixin' to die yet. Adults sing the blues. Blues adulthood means old enough to get the electric chair if you shoot a man in Memphis.

7. You can have the blues in New York City, but not in Brooklyn or Queens. You can't have the blues in Hawaii, Maine, Aspen, or anywhere in Canada. Hard times in Vermont or North Dakota are just a depression. Chicago, St. Louis, Memphis, New Orleans, and Kansas City are still good places to have the blues.

8. A man with male pattern baldness ain't the Blues. A woman with male pattern baldness is. Breaking your leg 'cause you were skiing is not the Blues. Breaking your leg 'cause a alligator be chomping on it is.

9. The following colours do not belong in the blues:

    a. violet b. beige c. mauve d. chartreuse e. Kelly green

10. You can't have the blues in an office or a shopping mall, the lighting is wrong.

11. Good places for the Blues:

    a. The highway b. the jailhouse c. the empty bed d. inside a boxcar (on the midnight train) e. on your porch 'cause your baby done changed the lock f. a smoky, dark, flea-bag bar.

Bad places:

    a. Ashrams. b. Gallery openings. c. weekend in the Hampton's. d. Barnes & Noble / Starbucks. e. Nordstrom's. f. a Golf Course.

12. No one will believe it's the blues if you wear a suit, unless you happen to be an old black man and if you slept in it.

13. Do you have the right to sing the blues?

    Yes, if: a. your first name is a southern state--like Georgia. b. You're older than dirt. c. You're blind. d. You actually did shoot a man in Memphis. e. You can't be satisfied.

No, if: a. You were once blind but now can see b. you're deaf. c. You have a trust fund, 401k or an IRA. d. The man in Memphis lived.

14. Neither Julio Iglesias, Barry Manilow, Anne Murray, Celine Dion, Britney Spears, nor Barbara Streisand can sing the blues (and it's illegal for them to try).

15. Blues is not a matter of colour. It's a matter of bad luck. Tiger Woods cannot sing the Blues. Sonny Liston could have. Ugly white people also got a leg up on the Blues especially if they were brought up in the projects.

16. If you ask for water and baby gives you gasoline, it's the blues.

    Other blues beverages are: a. Cheap wine b. Rotgut whiskey. c. Muddy water d. warm beer e. moonshine f. Black coffee

Blues beverages are NOT:

    a. Any mixed drink or "call brand" whiskey b. Any wine that is kosher for Passover c. Yoo Hoo (all flavours) d. Evian or Perrier e. cappuccino f. Slim Fast g. Snapple.

17. If it occurs in a cheap motel, smoky bar, or a shotgun shack, it's a blues death. Stabbed in the back or shot by a jealous lover is a blues way to die. So is the electric chair, substance abuse, lonely on a broken down cot, freezing in a boxcar on the southbound midnight train, or being denied treatment in an emergency room. It is not a blues death if you die during a tennis match or a liposuction treatment.

    Any combination of accepted ways to die is ok. So if you are freezin' on the southbound midnight train, stoned out yo' mind, bleedin' cause your baby done stabbed you in the back while you was messin' around, an' you fixin to die, that qualifies as a blues death.

18. Some Blues names for Women:

    a. Sadie b. Big Mama c. Bessie

19. Some Blues Names for Men

a. Joe b. Willie c. Little Willie (Not in the British sense because the English can't sing the blues.) d. Blind Willie e. Lightning

NOTE: Persons with names like Heather, Jason, Sierra, Michelle, Jean-Michel (or Jean-anything), Amber, Nigel, or Sequoia will not be permitted to sing the blues no matter how many men they shoot in Memphis.

20. Other Blues Names (a starter kit)

    a. Name of Physical infirmity (Blind, Cripple, Asthmatic) b. First name (see above) or name of fruit (Lemon, Lime, Apple, but not Kiwi) c. Last Name of President (Jefferson, Johnson, Fillmore, etc.)

21. I don't care how tragic your life is; if you own a computer, iPod, or palm pilot, you cannot sing the blues, period. Sorry.

22. Epitaph on a blues musician's tombstone:

    "I didn't wake up this morning"

CHAPTER 21: A CONSPIRACY THEORY

Who really has or is closest to the truth? Let's look at some figures.

1) If 2 people with opinions that are not in harmony claim to have the truth, 50% must be wrong?
2) If 10 similar people claim truth, at least 90% are wrong?
3) Should 100 people claim the truth, then at least 99% failure rate again!
4) Now with these types of stats, how are we meant to recognize that one illusive party standing out that is actually correct?

Before we start, please read through and test this email I received some time ago, it's arguably more than coincidence.

1) New York City has 11 letters
2) Afghanistan has 11 letters.
3) Ramsin Yuseb (The terrorist who threatened to destroy the Twin Towers in 1993 has 11 letters.
4) George W Bush has 11 letters.

This could be a mere coincidence, but this gets more interesting:
1) New York is the 11th state.
2) The first plane crashing against the Twin Towers was flight number 11.
3) Flight 11 was carrying 92 passengers. 9 + 2 = 11
4) Flight 77, which also hit Twin Towers, was carrying 65 passengers. 6+5 = 11
5) The tragedy was on September 11, or 9/11 as it is now known. 9 + 1 + 1 = 11
6) The date is equal to the US emergency services telephone number 911. 9 + 1 + 1 = 11.

Sheer coincidence? Read on and make up your own mind:

1) *The total number of victims inside all the hi-jacked planes was 254.*
   2 + 5 + 4 = 11.
2) *September 11 is day number 254 of the calendar*
   year. Again 2 + 5 + 4 = 11.
3) *The Madrid bombing took place on 3/11/2004.*
   3 + 1 + 1 + 2 + 4 = 11.
4) *The tragedy of Madrid happened 911 days*
   after the Twin Towers incident.

Now this is where things get totally eerie:
The most recognized symbol for the US, after the Stars & Stripes,
   is the Eagle. The following verse is taken from the Quran, the
   Islamic holy book: "For it is written that a son of Arabia would
   awaken a fearsome Eagle. The wrath of the Eagle would be
   felt throughout the lands of Allah and lo, while some of the
   people trembled in despair still more rejoiced, for the wrath of
   the Eagle cleansed the lands of Allah and there was peace."
That verse is number 9.11 of the Quran.

Still unconvinced about all of this..?
Open Microsoft Word and do the following:

1. *Type in capitals Q33 NY. This is the flight number of the first plane to*
   hit one of the Twin Towers.
2. *Highlight the Q33 NY.*
3. *Change the font size to 48.*
4. *Change the font to WINGDINGS. You should get this:*

What do you think now?!

Now let's look at those who claim the truth. We have the following, but to name a few.

1) The Christians who are divided into Catholics, Protestants (go Ireland!), Anglicans, Methodists, NGK, and others of more traditional back ground, of which most had a war against another variation at some point or other. Killing each other for ultimate domination, oops, sorry – for the right to spread the ultimate truth that they exclusively posses.

2) Various Christian variations not recognized by "conventional Christians" such as Mormons, Jehovah Witnesses, Seventh Day Adventists, Amish, and others. At least the Jehovah Witnesses try to research history for the truth, unlike many Christians who claim to have it!

3) The more evangelical churches such as Pentecostal, His People, and Vineyard, where people shake, fall down in the spirit, and please do not use the word "hype". It's astounding at the miracles that have happened but the "converted" and/or "healed" all seem to disappear? Surely a valid resurrection would make front-page news? We had a TV documentary where the charismatic Bennie Hinn's "healed" majority conveniently all could not be traced. Then a few who had been found had died from the very illness Bennie cured. Did their families get a refund from Bennie? Also conveniently Bennie could not be reached for comment. Perhaps he was at the bank making a deposit? Just a thought!

4) The Eastern religions like Muslim, Hindu, and various other beliefs that subscribe to multiple Gods, or one Deity. These religions often being the strictest of all. I think many of these might be closer to the truth, but there's radicals who pervert ALL beliefs. Not to mention the promise of a few virgins for those who sacrifice themselves – the ultimate blow-up job? In their defense, most Eastern religions are also motivated to help, spread peace and care for the others. Not a bad ideal at all, provided you share their belief!.

5) The Jews, who are also not excused from sub-dividing. We have Orthodox, Modern and at least one or more other strains of "Gods chosen people". This nation has a biblical history of killing other nations in God's name, promoting the concubine

theory in B.C. time. Ever read the Old Testament? Killing was one of the main pastimes, then taking over the loser's animals, woman, etc. Good thing they weren't in Southern Africa around about a hundred years ago?

6) Spiritualists like John Edwards who "cross over" and chat to the dearly departed. Surely if the dead were talking a lot more of us would hear them. Isn't it rather arrogant to believe that one in millions can hear the dead. And assuming John's actually credible, why doesn't he ask a suicide bomber if they were rewarded – it certainly would be assuring to know if their efforts were in vane or not? Or even say "hi" to Jimi Hendrix and ask if he's still jamming? Come on John, give us something really interesting!

7) Tribal beliefs as found in native Africans as well as the American Indians, again I'm sure that with the right research we could find once more several "denominations". Hey what happened to the Incas? Facts now people, not more theories and/or philosophies!

8) Then we have the atheists. We cannot really blame these people; religion hasn't really given them something to believe in. A friend of mine had this tongue in cheek phrase, "Thank God I'm an atheist!"

9) Those who believe in Holistic options, (and the list continues!)

Our divisions are not restricted to religious beliefs only; there are so many political parties in each country on the 5 continents that the call of the day is division! Weird concept, each division exists to try an unite people, sort of like going forward in reverse?

In our country for example we have the ANC (Another Negative Combination)), the DA (the Desperate Alliance?), PAC (Pointless And Clueless?), and God knows what else. Then we have constant splits in these factions as they swap parties and change opinions faster than a woman changes her choice of clothes! Every party claims to know the ONLY way to save its nations problems. There's not a country exempt from politics, if there were, we'd all probably immigrate to it?

The scary part here is that as we add these groups to the list so the percentage of those who MUST be wrong becomes proportional negative to there actually being an absolute truth.

Now the problem I have is that most denominations spring from finding out that the previous society/religion was perverting the "truth" for their own worldly gain such as wealth, power, and luxuries.

Similarly some are formed as a result of not being able to pervert them, so new directions are formed to line their pockets with. Most sects, if I may call the above options this, rely on money for their leaders existence. And most often we find these leaders living in the lap of luxury. Let's explore this.

We have the Pope – the Vatican has enough treasure that can be sold to feed the poor for years, yeah go Catholics! Billy Graham has millions in his bank balance, remember folks, there's a big difference between kneeling down and bending over! The screaming, rather plumpish leader of the Rhemar Church, Pastor Ray Mc Cauly who's wife was in magazines flaunting her jewelry while her and her husband live in a mansion, paid for by the congregation, of which the majority live in the shadow of this.

Yeah I know I've shown this cartoon before, but I really think it deserves a second display. If not for any other reason but to reinforce the message of business side of living for now vs. our eternal life-after-death investment!

The NG Kerk (of South Africa) has their collector knocking on our door every month asking for money, has exercised his right to offer criticism, but not once as I recall offered help or asked how our spiritual life was! Nope, no concern if God was active in our life, just open that wallet folks, the pastor has to pay for his new car!

Now some Eastern Muslim strains will send their followers to blow themselves up, or "fly you to your office"(Sep 11 flight tragedy), while the leader sits, or rather hides. There's believing in your cause, brainwash the masses to do your dirty work. Nice, real nice.

With more research we could write pages about all the above sects, their strengths and weaknesses, and how some leader or other has tarnished the belief, or led to lack of credibility. The sad part is how the human species will allow themselves to be indoctrinated into following charismatic leaders, which sometimes costs them their lives while the leader sits in comfort, or runs away from the responsibility of his commands to the mindless sheep that obey him.

Now here we get to the beginning of my conspiracy theory. Let's assume there's an elite family or group of people that actually run our planet, perhaps the secret society called the "Illuminati" – seen the movie Tomb Raider? The best way to dominate someone is to pacify him or her, or to demotivate them. Lowering their ability to think for themselves and rather encourage memory as opposed to creativity can do this. Just for your own interest, type the word "illuminati" into your internet browser and be prepared to be surprised!

Look how the world is going, the TV entertains most of us, we no longer have to think! We're bombarded with negative numbing visions of violence, murder, suing, hatred, anger, soapies, and war! In the minority are a few comedies and escape movies such as sci-fi. But these are often scoffed at as they're not "real life".

Yep, they, (whoever they are) want us to watch others suffer real life trauma, and degrade anything that require a sense of imagination. Perhaps the idea is for us to believe that our lives are not sooo bad as those witnessed on the screen? This in turn will hopefully help us accept the often-wrong selfish decisions of our politicians and religious leaders. Don't the two often go hand in glove?

Here's a quick, humor filled, look at how these lads can keep us in the dark and fill us full of shit! You gotta love these emails. This email was circulating after the power failures began as a result of the lack of foresight regarding the power demands as needed in South Africa.

The government tried to cry 'sabotage' – just before elections! Then the main 'boss' of Eskom (the power dude) got interviewed on TV regarding his salary – does he deserve it after this scandalous happening? Conveniently no real answer was given, and the public is asked to compromise for the short sightedness of our 'wonderful (in)competent leaders! And the dude leading us into darkness? Well he still draws a HUGE salary that neither you nor I have ANY control over. In SA how can we NOT resign ourselves to a conspiracy theory of sorts?

Here's a few more jokes that sprang into action shortly after the Eksdom, oops, Eskom. (For the Afrikaans illiterate, 'Eksdom translated means "I'm dumb" while Eskom is the SA electricity company) Let's give the devil a break here, even he has more smarts!

And now for another email about the aftermath after the power failures, obviously the sewerage system went crazy and caused problems as a lack of power when everything stopped! Not to mention all the money lost from huge companies that rely on automation – none of these companies got compensated. It's amazing how our leaders sidestep their responsibilities.

Water vs. Alcohol

It has been scientifically proven that should we drink a liter of water every day, so that at the end of a year you would of consumed more than a kilogram of escherichia coli bacteria. This is the same bacteria as found exclusively in shit, yep, human excrement! (This is found in the water, which we drink daily)

Now if we consume brandy, rum, whiskey, vodka or even beer, the alcohol, which is present prevents these bacteria due to the filtration system that is subjected to. With this in mind I must point out that I'd rather drink alcohol and talk shit, than to drink water and be full of shit!

The human race is a wonderful species, especially those who hunger for riches and power. What better way to get rid of competition than by numbing them, or getting them to conform to society? We spend our first 12 years learning to conform at school.

The present school syllabus focuses more on memory and formulae than actually teaching how to think. The aim to get the student onto the way of "what to think". South Africa now wants to make more languages a compulsory subject. So after we speak these various languages, what will actually have to share, other than being able to watch TV in several languages and order a pizza in them – jeez, can you imagine the sub titles in 11 official languages, there won't be space left for the picture?

Will there be time left for thinking? What happened to chess, cluedo, and other wonderful thinking and strategy games? Trivia pursuit gives the winner a pat on the back for knowledge. I'd rather have less knowledge, and the most wisdom to apply what I do know. Trivia pursuit and other games growing in popularity are memory games, which reinforce my belief that wisdom is only really exercised by those who wish to control us.

Yes, you're a genius if you know who jumped a certain height in 1954 at an Olympic game, but a scientist is often depicted as a nerd for actually thinking.

Let's face it, bullies often make their way to the top, those who often make it to the top might not do so as a result of brute force, but know how to manipulate their fellow less motivated, or rather less intellectual peers. Many of us dislike confrontation – this is the bully's ideal scenario.

Keep the underdog down, but give him just enough to let him think he is okay and that he shouldn't complain. And some where on the human food chain as we near the top is this secret conspiring group that perhaps creates a working and social environment through rules via religions to keep the average plebb in place. The last thing our world's leaders want is to be questioned?

Mankind wants to marry, procreate, succeed at something and grow. By numbing relationships – eventually we're back to **nymph to nun** – they help mankind try and struggle with his and hers first priority – relationships and family. We're flooded by one man, one-woman relationships, mmm, this wasn't so 2000 years plus ago in the bible? Or in some non-western cultures where divorce was seldom, if ever mentioned? Our TV gives us perfect "idols" and movie stars who we sometimes compare our spouses against. If not, the TV still provides a fashion for not communicating.

Sex is also what drives many people. What better way to screw up relationships than to make people too self-aware? "My goodness, I'm too fat", so the soon to be anorexic starves themselves to try and be cosmetically appealing before they think they're presentable to enjoy, or even have sex.

The idols TV reality music focuses primarily on cosmetic first, then the ability to sing. What does the age limit imply too, that if we're 30+, we're just that bit too old, or unacceptable to market? This is true for beauty pageants to!

TV is telling us continuously to "drop a size". It's no wonder that many woman have a problem with sex when trying to live up to be the ideal woman. And men are equally to blame for often comparing their partners after being exposed to this method of comparison, and meeting the standard.

Not to mention the guilt when I struggle to see my beer tummy drive away and hide muscles that are a standard feature of most adverts on TV, as do many men that experience similar occurrences when over 35. I actually like myself until I'm reminded by TV of how society might like me to be, ironically I don't in any way want to look like Justin Timberlake, or Usher.

Then we have the unrealistic "great sex scenes" on TV, that make many feel inadequate with the conventual's "missionary position". Let alone the clothing and lifestyles enjoyed by many seen in movies. As humans we often compare ourselves, we're only human, and when we match ourselves against these model sex symbols it's difficult not to feel just a little inadequate. Many, if not most of these models haven't had children either.

Most couples I've noticed have great sex before children, and then it dies down after the family growth. When still "mating", couples go out more, enjoy less TV, and are possibly fitter, healthier, and more cosmetic appealing. Along comes the biological change, a child later, bodies stretched and tired we turn to TV for escape, only to be reminded that our bodies are different.

Instead of moving on to enjoy our blessing, TV often points out the "blandness" of married life. Ever watch "Married with children, the Simpson's, and other sitcoms?" Society and I are not on the same ideal journey; I wouldn't trade my children for this entire planet, with world peace thrown in! Although cheating on my wife for a sex life has crossed my mind, it's my choice to give my children a home with both biological parents, despite this loss of one of my greatest enjoyments.

Hey, just a quick step back, maybe if Homer Simpson was actually responsible for SA's power as in this joke I received below, we'd suffer fewer power breaks? Just a thought…

Eskom   Koeberg Nuclear Power Plant

**REACTOR MAINTAINANCE
HEAD OF MAINTAINANCE**

FRED SIMSON

002497

With cost of living inflating we are so stressed about our next month salary, we struggle to enjoy our partner, even occasionally blame them for lack of finances! Now who causes the increase in petrol, taxes, medical, and not to mention LEGAL costs when we want justice for whatever reason.

It certainly seems that there just **might** be a conspiracy to undermine, exploit, control, and prevent 99.9999% of the world population from reaching their true potential. Let's face it, when last did petrol, taxes, food, inflation ever really worry our political powers – oh that's right, they are the benefactor!

When shit happens, these benefactors merely sidestep and let the public take up the slack. My question is, "who controls them?" South Africa's currency value varies due to external factors such as the dollar, petrol, etc – now who decides these values?

Lastly, when last did George Bush, or Thabo Mbeki actually have to ride down a damaged road, or have someone harass them for money on a

Sunday afternoon, find that after a petrol increase it meant they couldn't buy their child new clothes (or for their spouse for that matter)?

Yep, these leaders really don't seem to realize the impact of their decisions, if they claim they do, then once more is there a conspiracy afoot? One thing I do know is that there's not a poor or even average politician on this planet, all the buggers drive luxury cars, have huge homes, and a sizeable bank balance, it really seems that they look after their needs first!

Who do they answer to?

Time line comments:
After I personally got let down by our wonderful politically established systems I took the liberty to email two political parties. My question was "What percentage of SA actually took the time and effort to actually vote, in my book this is a reflection of who actually believe in the political system and those who run it. To no surprise, only 48% of those registered to vote of SA actually took the time to stand and make their X, that's right people, less than half of our REGISTERED population actually cares about the fate of SA.

Now if we assume that only half the population is actually registered, then the amount that voted decreases to 24%! Then assuming the ANC took 60 of that we have a possible 15% of the country that actually voiced their faith in Mbeki! You do the math folks; it's not rocket science. So when Mbeki said on TV he's popularity grew to 75% on TV, my question is: 75% of what? If it's 75% of the previously calculated 15%, then he has just over 10% backing him?

Shouldn't they introduce a rule where if more than half the country doesn't vote the present party gets fired due to lack of faith or interest from the population? This might just inspire the political powers to actually take an interest in their countries future.

The bully theory is now reinforced as we still pay tax towards these lads as they lead us into darkness.

Chapter 22: The "Smarter" Nymph Glands

This chapter is bound to spark further racial and social issues, although this is not the intention.

The purpose of this chapter:
To see if some people are not perhaps more gifted than others. This means that some Nymph gland owners are able to understand and approach life with better insight as a result of what they've been exposed to, or as a result of the gene pool from which they come.

Now before I go further let me explain my approach to various cultures from another angle.

1) I do not think it is right for any one culture to enforce itself onto another culture, or even merge the two together with the one absorbing the other. If you want to merge, let others still enjoy their original one – never take away something that is important to someone, unless it's destructive to others. If they can exist in their own surrounding without hurting you, let them – this approach could possibly of cancelled many a war!

2) No culture has the right to think that they are superior, although there are different levels of awareness and understanding in various social circles. This is reflected in their cultures accomplishments. Read the following chapter "Are all races equal?"

3) Each culture has an exception; all groups have great people and idiots on either side of the "average" spectrum. We too often generalize a culture which I'm sure has also sparked too many a

war, and given reason for even more politicians to find a reason to walk the earth preying on the gullibility of its inhabitants.

4) If we respected each other's values as established in their culture and didn't criticize them, or continued to let them have their space, we might have a lot less conflict.

Now we **do** judge various cultures, we **do** have this desire to find out where we stand in the food chain, and to justify our social standing. We then end up tramping on others. Blame this on the human ego. Here are a few comments that motivate this statement, not that I necessarily think that it's right. In the chapter about love I ventured to state that "we have clever and stupid people", bare with me before you hurl this book out the window and think about these facts.

1) Health and nutrition experts have informed us that diets can effect our mind; maybe that's how the term "food for thought" came about? And go speak to a dietician and learn how many 3rd world cultures have diets that are not prone to motivate help the brain be stimulated Now in my country we have a predominant 3rd world nation that has elected a government to run it, yes the majority successful voters are largely the owners of undeveloped mental capabilities. I'm not suggesting that malnutrition is a racist sin, it's a shame! They never get to reach the potential within themselves. Please I am not insulting them, simply stating a fact.

Here's a quick cultural giggle, another one of the many emails received.

*After digging to a depth of 100 metres last year, **Russian** scientists found traces of copper wire dating back 1000 years, and came to the conclusion that their ancestors already had a telephone network one thousand years ago.*

*So, not to be outdone, in the weeks that followed, **American** scientists dug 200 metres and headlines in the US papers read: "US scientists have found traces of 2000 year old optical fibre, and* *have concluded that their ancestors already had advanced high-tech digital telephone 1000 years earlier than the Russians."*

*One week later, an **African** newspaper reported the following: "After digging as deep as 500 metres, Zulu scientists have found absolutely nothing. They have concluded that 5000 years ago, their ancestors were already using wireless technology."*

I must say now that democracies are great in an ideal world, but not a realistic solution. Think about this, if you had three or more children in a family, would they determine their sleeping times, their clothing, diet, approach to schooling? No, the adults make these decisions, even though they're now in the minority, the adults are still responsible for the success of the family – no space for democracy in large families are there? So we must learn two valuable lessons here.

1) The head of the family must be respected and trusted.
2) The trust placed in the head of the family is to justified and earned.

Let us parallel this to our country; the previous government messed up lifting their culture over that of the local inhabitants. They were the adults enjoying the wisdom to their own benefit at the expense of the children, the majority. We (the minority) were lead to believe we were superior beings, where we should of rather acknowledged that our culture was lucky enough to have developed better through better diet habits. I apologize for this.

Again, PLEASE, if you doubt these words, go talk to a dietician and see if the solution to a healthy brain is mielie pap! Similarly do some research on the effects of malnutrition. I believe that the first four years of development are crucial to the adult years; with incorrect nutrition the future adult is almost doomed to mediocrity! (Yes I know there are a few, very few exceptions – please name one?)

So the oppressed got miffed, hey so would I, and this gave the greedy manipulating politicians a reason to blame the previous culture for it's failure and reverse the order of things – South Africa calls this "affirmative action".

To summarize:

1) A child's diet in it's first few years determine the efficiency of it's understanding. The processing power so to speak of it's brain. This in turn affects the nymph gland owner too, hence the title of this chapter. If you doubt this, please consult the medical profession.

2) The average, more tribal African does not have a diet that can promote healthy competitive thinking the same way many European cultures do.

3) The result, most African countries are in trouble, with the like of Robert Mugabe, and previous fellows like Idiot, I mean Idi Amin. (Uganda) Dictating the nations demise. If you were to compare the African continent economies to those of Europe or North America you would find the result to support this theory.

4) Western cultures have produced great minds like Einstein, Bell, Edison – people with creative "genius", name one African inventor!

5) This does not make the people bad, they are simply disadvantaged due a to lack of capacity to understand, much the same way a child is.

6) A democracy can only work if ALL concerned are equally enlightened and have a similar ability to think creatively.

Now let's again return to our original topic,
The long walk to nun gland, or the death of the nymph gland. Those that can see the future of our country are concerned about opportunities of our children. Now if we're to procreate, how do we expect our spouses to do so when they are sincerely worried about the future of the fruit of their loins? How do we expect the nymph gland to function under these concerns?

And even if their nearsightedness or unwillingness allows them to deny the possibility of a corrupt government, they are still faced by an increase in living. The nymph gland bearer still has to try and find out how to afford all its clothes, food, and education for children and so much more. Face it folks, stress kills sex - go nun gland!

Ask yourself this "One jet that our government purchased, at about R15million, would of paid for how many children's education?" – think about this before you vote again! It's in any government's best interest to offer hope and attain a fine balance or rather an illusion of progress. This way they maintain control with little chance of being challenged, and if so the dissatisfied voter more than likely hasn't the means, or effort to see his comments through!

The stresses in South Africa for many average workers are that government policies threaten their source of income, similarly the increase of petrol and other goods, not to mention the tollgate scenarios.

Although the modern South African spouse is not necessarily aware of these government occurred expenses they do feel the aftermath, the increases in living, medical availability, higher crime rates, corrupt police, (Hey, these guys are just trying to feed their families too!) and so much more. This is not conducive to a healthy nymph gland.

The promise of Utopia to the Children of South Africa helps the procreation process with the struggling, once pushed aside cultures. Notice how population growth of the whites differs from the blacks? Interesting, don't you think?

I dare to venture that little has changed, and possibly the slight shift in our countries direction has perhaps still not been beneficial to the country as a whole, with the rich simply getting richer and raising the bread line in the process. My hearts cries for ALL the children who lose their rights to have a fair chance at life.

Who suffers? All of us; the nymph gland owners and those that miss the nymph gland in their partner.

The result? A frustrated, insecure nation that blames their spouses instead of the origin of perhaps too many of our problems, the bullies in power.

I listed some financial facts from the nation wide magazine "Huisgenoot" date 17th March 2005. Here is evidence of the priorities of the ANC. The purchase of the Grippon jet fighter was made against advice of the air force; I wonder how many others the government ignored?

1) **Hawk Training jets** - 25 in total at R2 500 000. This could of paid for 2500 policeman for 10 years. No wonder our crime is so high!

2) **Agusta helicopters** – 30 in total at R2 500 000. The salaries for 1700 doctors over 10 years could also have been accommodated. Maybe SA hasn't got a medical problem? Yeah right!

3) **Super Lynx helicopters** – 4 at R1 100 000. At Swartklip the production of ammunition has caused life-threatening pollution. The workers get a whopping R1000 compensation. I guess this is all the working population is worth to our politicians?

4) **Airbus aircraft** – at least 8 are ordered with another 6 pending – at about R12 000 000 each. This financial injection could help rehabilitate about 1000 000 street children. Provide them with physical and emotional help and get them a basic education.

5) **Corvette warships** – 4 at R6 000 000. This could replace 250 000 squatter hovels with basic house. This in turn would also create employment for the builders – about 90 000 people might have a job according to Huisgenoot figures.

6) **Submarines** – 3 at R4 500 000. We could provide for 6 years free education. But maybe the powers that be feel our educational systems are great. We simply just push more students per teacher and the state dignitaries can also afford new cars.

7) **Gripen fighter jets** – 28 were ordered at R15 000 000. Well this amount could of supplied enough antiretroviral drugs for 400 000 AIDS positive people in our land. But at an average of

1300 dying from AIDS each day there'll probably no one left to defend us against in the future? Maybe Zuma can supply each with a free bar of soap and a shower?

I also find it odd that a submarine is twice the price of a Ferrari! Surely the size, technology, hi-tech equipment, labor and so much more that went into killing someone from under water is more than twice that of the aforementioned car?

I had to include this email joke I received. Just a reminder folks, ALL this emails were sent to me unsolicited, although I do enjoy them. The attitude being the same as one might share a humor with a friend.

How smart is this mans glands? And to think he now wants to runs South Africa and was once 2nd in charge!

Sleep well Mr. President…

Chapter 23: Are All Races Equal?

Well I'm sure this will get many racist minds turning over various ethical and moral issues and implications. I hope I don't get banned or locked up for these comments!

My intent is to further provoke the previous chapter's debate from a curios, questioning and calculated stand, not an emotional one. Too many people have killed each other as a result of heated emotions! Before I go further we I'd like to entertain this thought. What exactly is a racist? I've learnt there are two opinions, each with a certain germ of logic.

a)   Is a racist some one who likes his own race and is proud of his heritage, culture, beliefs, and background? They do not hate other races or put them down, they simply prefer their own. If so, they're not a bad person, what do you think?

b)   Or is he a fanatical purist who hates other races and puts down other cultures, as he believes he is superior, doesn't respect other cultures, dismisses other beliefs simply as "wrong" and inferior? Yeah, well this fellow needs some attitude adjustment!

Well if your answer is 'a)', then being a racist is not a bad thing, as embracing who you are and where you're from does NOT mean you believe yourself to be superior!

Try thinking along these lines, a tennis player and a soccer player are two completely different sportsmen. There is little in common regarding team work, rules, sports equipment, etc... Now replace the word "sports" with 'race' and we can safely compare that the tennis players prefer their own race! (Or sport)

This does not mean the tennis player thinks he is better than a soccer player, he has simply chosen a sport that he prefers. There's even a good chance the tennis player likes watching soccer, or even plays for fun when not engaging his personal preference.

Hey, did you know South Africa really has an unspoken attitude towards our local taxi drivers and their attitude to safety and road rules. These two cartoons sum up the silent attitudes towards them, not to mention the possible underlying racial implications that might accompany them!

Kleptomania is often associated with the taxi culture, not to mention the safety features.

This one is a personal favorite mocking both the policing policies in our country as well the validity of many of our countries taxi drivers. Please observe the hinted implications regarding the skin color of the taxi driver. I'm surprised the above cartoons are legal, and not regarded as hate speech or whatever.

Now what really miffs me are the bullies of the world that love to twist situations for their own selfish agendas. In South Africa we have the Apartheid stigma from the past that haunts us still today. The more the government says we're all equal the more they enforce that certain races MUST enjoy preference when it comes to race, not ability! They call this "affirmative" action.

You're going to enjoy this spoof at the desperate attempt for work by the rather not bright lad below. Maybe it's closer to the truth than we care to mention?

[Frikkie is a typical Afrikaans 'white' male name.]

Reconciliation structures are put in place to forgive, but we keep reminding each other of past sins and make many who are not guilty pay for previous governments crimes? How does a sore heal if we keep picking at the scab? Is racism in this context dead, or a tool for success with a certain level of ambiguity depending on the level of convenience for the user?

What's really amazing is that we never hear on ground level who gets to decide what the HUGE salaries of these newly appointed politicians are, similarly those who take over management, etc.. Come on lads, who decides their value, themselves or the country?

Land claims are used to ensure votes to a flailing government by those who do not have skills to farm or manage, holding those whose forefathers apparently plundered guilty and reintroducing an unfair reprisal by costing those who are NOW feeding the present generations of ALL races, their homes.

In short, farmer X's great grandfather in 1900(and whatever) purchased land legally under a wrong government law. (Wrong by today's standards.) Over a century later the new government has just short of reversed this situation reclaiming land to people with no skills, thus costing those with the knowledge their home.

What no-one seems to mention on our local TV is that when the whole system eventually falls apart, as it is doing in Zimbabwe, those who made these decisions will be happily retired on YOUR tax money, and probably importing food from USA, Europe, or Asia. That's assuming they even still live in our land. That's right folks, it's easy to make promises to get power, then pass the buck to the next while retiring without the problems experienced by those who ensured their pension!

No wonder the nymph glad kicks in for starting families in SA, once the reality of family provision kicks in, the stress and worry pushes many married peoples sex life into oblivion. How does the programming of the intelligent mind run with confidence when exposed to fear of a dubious future and the looming reality of a possible loss? How do they provide for their children? And then with pensions schemes looking a bit gray, how do we provide for ourselves?

Well, what about our rapidly expanding lower income community? Well, these poor people are promised the world and have little to loose. We could argue that they are the 'children' of our country? Are these the people that need the most help? Can we treat them as equal peers, or rather as **equal human beings** that have not reached intellectual maturity that you and I PERHAPS MIGHT enjoy? Or will this attitude remove them from the voting lists of those that wish to exploit their social condition and status?

Just a thought folks, you need to answer this for yourself, please don't lay any moral, ethic or racial guilt side steps on me. All I know is that maybe we could learn from some Eastern culture (China & Japan) regarding population monitoring and the success coupled with it.

Let's return to the topic of us all being equal, despite race creed, or country. What has history taught us about our pride, ethical awareness, conscience driven species, and the homosapien? Well in biblical times we killed each other to ensure the stronger tribe surviving, although religious leaders claimed it God's will. If history is accurate we were trying to exercise some form of genocide in Germany too a century ago – and religious leaders claimed God's will for BOTH sides.

Before our little country was exposed to the Dutch and other Europeans 1600 and something, the Africans were also warring one tribe against another – exercising some lack of moral obligation to their fellow man. If I recall correctly our first settlers only encountered the Xhosa and/or Zulu hundreds of kilometers away, over a certain river up North. The poor Bushmen and Strand Looper, the only really passive nations, have suffered almost extinction! What race are most our politicians and who really deserves compensation for wrong doings and from whom? Mmm!

Hey what about the American Indians, isn't that sort of quite similar scenario to what happened here, or is it a level of convenience to turn a blind eye under the 'fine print' that USA never had the name 'Apartheid', thus making it cool to rather redirect and appease their own conscience by focusing on our sins? And shouldn't we research the Australian Aborigines, or will this open another moral and ethic debate while other nations look to us to escape their own guilt? Didn't America and Australia's "white" population all come from the same continent as South Africa? I'm under the impression we all originated from Europe.

What puzzles me the most is that it is okay for us to terminate our own species when we're the same color in the name of war, but should our skins be a different shade – all hell breaks loose!

Enough of this and let's look at various cultures and the evolutionary path they have followed. It seems that basic items such as the wheel, combustion engines as in your car, electricity, radio, telephone, use of gas, ships, all stemmed from European, or rather Western cultures. I don't recall reading ANY-WHERE about any Western explorer being greeted by another nation be it Africa, America, Australia, etc... in a car! Or, that they were welcomed via radio in advance. No lights were switched on to help welcome them into something as old as a harbor, nope, no harbors pre 1652 in Southern Africa folks – all the explorer's ships left from one, but were they ever welcomed into one?

With this in mind is it correct to assume that some cultures or civilizations were more advanced. And in being advanced is it also correct to assume that they had to be superior and this was manifested in their inventions and personal drive to improve their standards of living.

Another milestone for humanity is their artistic side, for example opera's, theatre, etc. Europe has many throughout the countries while I would like to know of any existing pre1652 in Southern Africa? Did the same level of artwork go into a cave wall as went into the Mona Lisa?

Then we have our architecture to prove our civilized side. Both European and Asian cultures excelled in this, not to mention Northern Africa, especially Egypt. As well as mythical concepts what happened to the Inca's and some of South American cultures. These lads could BUILD folks! But the complexity in a grass and mud hut – you decide the level of initiative and attitude here...

To summarize here it seems as if we might be able to say that some cultures, or heaven forbid the use of the word 'races' might have progressed at different speeds. Could we then say that intelligence levels vary between cultures or that doomed bad word 'races'? Is mankind as a whole really equal?

One of our countries main gripes is that Apartheid held back development – and yes it most certainly did on many, but not ALL levels! We cannot argue this, BUT who held back development before then, in fact who held back development before 1652? Who can we blame for lack of evolving in Africa then? This opens another portal to this argument. What if our African cultures did not want to evolve? The answer that springs to mind is this, and I think it deserves a paragraph.

Should a culture not wish to evolve, why would it so badly want to be part of the other culture that has developed electricity, cars, communication methods, ships, planes, etc.. Why don't they rather shun this and revert back to what made them happy before they were exposed to this. By wanting to be on par it would almost seem as if the less developed culture has realized it has not progressed as others have. (Why though? Was it choice or inability to evolve? I'm not going to answer this because I don't know, even though I have a few opinions I'd rather not voice)

Remember that no one came and taught Western culture how to make the wheel, invent electricity, and all other neat things previously mentioned. And if aliens were helping us back then – where are they now, maybe frozen in Roswell?

It's very difficult for me to believe that we're all equal. Even as a white SA male, I find different levels of intelligence in other of my own type and age group. This is manifested in quickness to understand, depth of thought, drive to progress and further ourselves. So if there are differences in my own culture, surely there MUST be differences in ability between cultures too!

I do not believe it's a crime to be superior or inferior. It's how we handle our own individual abilities towards those around us that make us 'humane'. Too often we lay blame at others feet, or play on ethical and moral feelings to escape our own inabilities, or to further our own path. We need to remember that no matter how clever we think we are, we can still learn something from our less gifted counterparts.

I believe it right for the superior to share should they wish to, but not to oppress and exploit others with their progress. Similarly the less gifted should not expect or hold a grudge against those with the ability to achieve more.

If they do then I should have license to carry a grudge against any one that has excelled more than me? Sort of like winning a race, and the lad that came second cries "unfair" as the winner was simply better than him. Shame, the lad that came second didn't have as powerful muscles, or perhaps he couldn't strategize his game as well as the victor? But he still beat how many others?

It's our genetic engineering that largely determines where we finish, and this is not a crime. Enjoy who you are and realize there's always better, and worse than you.

Now intelligence is a weird concept. Our leading scientists are attributed with a large level of the intelligent gene. While no one seems to ask where is the intelligence in greed, or building some-thing that can obliterate mankind with just a flick of a switch. Hey, that's real genius, build the life destroying bomb! So who really is superior, or should we say 'smarter than the average bear' as Yogi bear would say.

This goes to prove there is a HUGE difference between intelligence and wisdom. The first could be more tunnel vision, while the latter definitely considers the long-term 'bigger' picture.

Perhaps the animal kingdom has some clues, or at least ideas to banter with. The strongest survives here, but animals have little or no ethics, or even a soul some say, but do they ensure the survival of the species without conscience? You can answer this one. As the great guitarist Steve Vai wrote in one of his songs, "We're all human, but we're still animals."

And my newly acquired puppy is certainly a lot more forgiving, loving, understanding then many humanoids that walk this earth – go Cosmo, go. (Cosmo is the name of my dog) If only more people would accept each other so honestly and be quick to forgive we might just have a shot at heaven on earth between all races?

You'll also notice my attitude has changed from my opening paragraphs in the pets and relationships chapter. As mentioned there is a time line in this book.

CHAPTER 24: NYMPH GLAND INFLUENCES

After the past few chapters we need to review on what possibly influences the nymph gland to withdraw from active service. We need to realize that the choice to hibernate might be a subconscious decision, not as a result of our mate maliciously deciding to withhold sex from their partner. Here are some of the reasons that might cause the nymph gland to decline its position:

Please note these reasons are not in order of priority, and each nymph gland owner has their own unique combinations surrounding their personal world. Remember folks; we are not designed to multi task as efficiently as we would like to believe we can. When something is bugging us, there a reasonable chance that sex might be the last thing on our mind.

Although the poor lad below seems to be responding, or rather suffering from some physical disorder as a result of his programming malfunctioning. We can only speculate the cure might be the exposure to a healthy active nymph gland?

Some of these topics have been discussed in greater depth, and this chapter is simply meant to be an overview, or rather a check list should we be curious to the cause of our partners Nun gland being too active.

Career stress:
A lousy career, or job, can drain us mentally, emotionally and physically. When we're tired and irritable it's very easy to release this frustration on our partner as they are expected to simply understand us. When this occurs, the attacked person adopts some sort of retaliation, which is not conducive to a romantic evening. If your job sucks, it's your responsibility to do something about it! So to the stress sufferer – it's okay to be tired and pissed off, but if you let yourself be "pissed on" for too long you really only have yourself to blame.

For those who live with unhappy job sufferers, please try and understand and encourage them to realize they can change to a career. Find a quiet time and chat about options, maybe even see a career councilor. Both boys and girls screw up their chances of screwing here, not just the nymph gland carriers.

Financial stress:
This is often linked to career stress, if our salary sucks, at least make sure you enjoy the job. Job satisfaction can often make up for poor wages, but this does not make it acceptable. The lack of money in any family situation can cause untold problems such as poor diets, lack of clothing, no provision for after school education, not being able to participate in sports, peer pressure, social standing insecurities.

Hey maybe our currency might have these values in later years? For those familiar with SA terms, the word 'buggeroli' means 'nothing'. The train with the gravy being poured over it symbolizes the 'gravy train' scam from a few yeas ago. Some think it's still steaming ahead!

Many women also place the entire burden of financial provision at the feet of the male. I'm not entirely convinced if this is fair of them, although I do accept many males might be slack at trying to provide. Now to both partners in any marriage, you chose them as much as they chose you; no one had a gun at either one's head. So don't be too quick to criticize your spouse's choices, look who they married! You decided to be a team, so make sure you both understand at the beginning who is responsible for what, and also the consequences that might come along with any compromise.

Again both boys and girls have failed here in certain situations.

Political influences:
If you've read this book from the beginning you should realize that my opinion of this breed of human throw back is rather low. These people, especially South Africa's, have little if any idea of the impact of their decisions. They prioritize war ships and fighter planes while their rescue helicopters shut down one by one. They spend millions on new parliament buildings while the bulk of their nation still lives in shacks. They rely on your tax money to pay for services like police, the taxes are obviously not redistributed correctly, so the public has to hire security companies – our tax does efficiently cater for our government's new cars though, and the legal fees to defend these people, and their entertainment budgets! And the campaigns to convince those who cannot think for themselves to blame previous governments to sidestep their own wrong doings. Take the lad below, and his level of convenient lack of knowledge.

Now how do we expect our spouses to not get stressed at these truths, and ignore the existence of corrupt politicians? The fruit of their deeds is crime, murder, corruption, petrol increasing, food prices climbing, affirmative career options, dim future for the next generations – it's not a surprise that relationships struggle when those in them need to survive and provide first. Here boys and girls suffer at the hands of arrogant political mongers!

Co-existence in the same home:
I'm still confused regarding this topic with sincerest non-lustful motivation. Please re-read the chapter on the concubine theory. Having two people having to come home after a day in our new modern world is tough. We enjoyed the mating game so much when we had our own domiciles, now it's an issue if boys forget to lower the toilet seat, and glares when we have tampon wrappers on the basin. Not to mention forgetting to replace the toilet paper roll – see below!

Perhaps males are too flippant here, as their priorities differ. Woman tend to want to maintain a clean living condition and are not to concerned how the house is afforded, while men focus on the house bond and find an underpants on the shower tap quite trivial!

This I experienced from many males - their wives want the best, but don't realize the time needed to spend to earn the money to maintain such a life style. Similarly men do not realize hygiene implications of bum hair on the bath soap – face it folks, separate tents are not a bad solution! Can we really expect girls to think like boys, and vice versa?

Tiredness, lack of sleep:
Our bodies are dependent on a rest time. This is an issue for me, I LOVE my work/career and hate the experience of my body saying "time to sleep". Now any medical professional will explain at length the affects of sleep deprivation. The buggers are right too. My psychiatrist explained to me how our brain cells have a fluid around them, when we stress or are exhausted the fluid retreats into the cell to sustain the cells life

The hassle is that the fluid is used to conduct information from one cell to the next, which results in our awareness. (Woo hoo, go the human machine theory I enjoy) When our awareness is in jeopardy we can experience hallucinations, voices, and God knows what else. This is what happened to me. So I either entertained a spiritual manifestation or my brain was messed. After the correct medication I returned to normal. You decide if God or an Angel called me or I suffered a physical deficiency of sorts?

Inconsiderate partners:
On the whole I'd like to believe that the majority of those furless primates called "humans" are really quite nice. Most of us like to help, and are often fearful now days of being taken advantage of due to the society we live in. I also think most of us like the idea of loving someone, and taking care of them. But every now and then we have throwbacks. Now do something right and we never remember, screw up and we never forget! This generalization is sadly quite accurate.

So what I'm saying is that we might doubt too many people's honestly good intentions due to a handful who are actually mentally ill, or choose to be simply nasty. Well if we watch enough soapies we can validate the corrupt human nature, and by reading the news papers the politicians reinforce the possible accuracy of my faith in the average person.

Mental illness:
If the body malfunctions such as cancer, we have sympathy for the person. But should our infinitely more complex brain produce incorrect proportions of chemicals we tend to avoid the person, perhaps label them insane, and hold them responsible for their actions.

Both boys and girls suffer from this in the limited situations that they do occur in.

Physical illness, diseases:
The emotional stress of living with someone who has a terminal or handicapped physical condition adds to the list of problems. I've also witnessed the effects of illness on a child with Down syndrome on a family. If you were God would you test anyone to see if they were "worthy" to deal with this?

It's so easy to be an armchair player in the game of life. Same as those "experts" who comment on how the international team lost a game due to being "stupid". HELLO PEOPLE !!! Does anyone intentionally make his or her name ass? Does a team or person intentionally sit down and plan how they're going to navigate a course of disaster? – NO! But still, finding fault and having the solution for someone's errors is so much easier, and it provides too many armchair participants with a self importance by knowing the correct answer AFTER watching the game. By letting the time line pass to after the match, the observer prevents the opportunity to have his opinions proved wrong.

Similarly the average person does not want to be a burden on the one they love, when shit happens the stresses are awful! No one is at fault here; the way we deal with it holds the key to success.

Relocating:
Moving is one of the greatest stressful instances many psychologists will tell us. Makes sense, we might be moving away from friends and loved

ones with a familiarity to an area you called home! I think men might be more career driven on average than females. So it's safe to assume that the bi-brained half of us are more than likely going to push for a move to improve on living conditions for him and his mate.

The nymph gland holder now stands to follow and by doing so, looses contact with previously mentioned people and has to rebuild a home. No wonder the gland in question suffers! It's not rocket science. But the feminine half should realize the motivation behind her spouse and if the sacrifices do not justify the forward move, proceed to debate together about the pro's and con's regarding the idea. Make a joint decision before moving.

Alcohol and/or drug abuse:
When either the boy or girl chooses to abuse these, a distorted reality is created through abuse of the previously mentioned "stimulants". The guilt and responsibility should lie with the user. I have difficulty justifying the reason for relying on these substances for a form of escape.

In short, there are many influences that cause the nymph gland to evolve into the nun gland. Is there a guaranteed solution? Not really, but trying to understand and help each other is arguably the best place to start!

Diets:
All doctors will agree a healthy body means a healthy mind. The confusing part is when these experts conflict. Perhaps the best guideline is to see what food is common to most doctors diet recommendations, and avoid the diet attitude below, although it does have some distorted logic.

A humor filled look at your health:
Q: I've heard that cardiovascular exercise can prolong life. Is this true?
A: Your heart is only good for so many beats, and that's it... don't waste them on exercise. Everything wears out eventually. Speeding up your heart will not make you live longer; that's like saying you can extend the life of your car by driving it faster. Want to live longer? Take a nap.

Q: Should I cut down on meat and eat more fruits and vegetables?
A: You must grasp logistical efficiencies. What does a cow eat? Hay and corn. And what are these? Vegetables. So a steak is nothing more than an efficient mechanism of delivering vegetables to your system. Need grain? Eat chicken. Beef is also a good source of field grass (green leafy vegetable). And a pork chop can give you 100% of your recommended daily allowance of vegetable products.

Q: Should I reduce my alcohol intake?
A: No, not at all. Wine is made from fruit. Brandy is distilled wine, tequila is made out of cactus, that means they take the water out of the fruity bit so you get even more of the goodness that way. Beer is also made out of grain. Bottoms up!

Q: How can I calculate my body/fat ratio?
A: Well, if you have a body and you have body fat, your ratio is one to one. If you have two bodies, your ratio is two to one, etc.

Q: Aren't fried foods bad for you?
A: YOU'RE NOT LISTENING!!! Foods are fried these days in vegetable oil. In fact, they're permeated in it. How could getting more vegetables be bad for you?

Q: Will sit-ups help prevent me from getting a little soft around the middle?
A: Definitely not! When you exercise a muscle, it gets bigger. You should only be doing sit-ups if you want a bigger stomach.

Q: Is chocolate bad for me?
A: Are you crazy? Cocoa beans--another vegetable!!! It's the best feel-good food around!

Q: Is swimming good for your figure?
A: Explain whales to me.

Q: Is getting in-shape important for my lifestyle?
A: Hey! 'Round' is a shape!

Well, I hope this has cleared up any misconceptions you may have had about food and diets.

Remember my happy little chums. Life should NOT be a journey to the grave with the intention of arriving safely in an attractive and well preserved body, but rather to skid in sideways - Chardonnay in one hand - chocolate coated strawberries in the other - body thoroughly used up, totally worn out, and screaming - WOO HOO! What a Ride!

CHAPTER 25: THE MALE NYMPH GLAND

Okay one and all, here's where I put myself up for ridicule. Although the word nymphomaniac is reserved for nymph holders, it seems that most men are arguably more consistent with their quest for dispersing their reproductive fluid. In this book I've used the word "willy" as the more polite name for a penis.

Many woman will say that men are ruled by their balls, well how do you think my balls feel about this?
Read this quick joke email.

1) *It isn't easy being a dick; I've got a head I can't think with.* Some women argue this!

2) *An eye I can't see out of.* Although it does respond well to touch!

3) *I have to hang around with two nuts all the time.* Yep, no psychologist in the world can help these two!

4) *My closest neighbour is a real asshole.* Can't argue that one, can you?

5) *My best friend is a pussy.* Well it does try to make this friendship two-way.

6) *Every time I get excited I throw up*! I'm not even going to comment on this fact!

To justify this concept, the existence of the male nymph gland, let's revisit biblical times when one man had several wives, not the other way around. And then as the "cherry on top" he also enjoyed a few concubines. If I recall correctly, any woman who entertained a few "husbands" was stoned to death?

In modern day, we still have various African, and Eastern cultures that still live by this 'one husband, many wives' ideal, and with reasonably good results too I'm lead to believe. Jeez, I would have to be born in a Western Christian culture – one man, one fanny!

Now what should we call our male equivalent? The "overdriven Organ"? Or perhaps "the Rabbit attachment?" (As I'm a guitarist in a band, perhaps I should reserve this name for a future band? "Rabbit Attachment", nice ring to it?) Yep our second "brain", as many woman see it, has it's own purpose with a strong mission to help the procreation process.

So what's the difference between the woman and male primal drive to breed? Well, it seems, and I speak under correction, that the male drive just never seems to shut down, or at least it takes a few more years before it heads for retirement!

This does not mean that all boys are horny little mammals in search of lustful fulfillment, although most men, myself included would be really happy if their chosen partner continued to share their desires until we need splints to help keep this attachment "erect". I'd like nothing better than to share this joy with my wife until all we can do is 'rock' in an rocking chair or swing on the porch of our home at a gray age where that's about all we can do together.

The problem occurs when our subconscious drive causes a frustration level that results in bitterness, resentment and other unpleasant attitudes towards the nymph life support system. Sadly there is a joke that explains that a woman is simply a "life support system for a fanny". In our defense I intercepted a female response saying, "Men are a life support system for a wallet!" (Remember everyone, we need to enjoy the humor behind these remarks, too much seriousness can also kill you!) The hormone is a terrible, confusing catalyst!

At this point I'd like to invite response from doctors, psychologists, psychiatrists, spiritual leaders and other human specialists to help me understand what the purpose is for this drive. My stereotyping conclusion is that there are bound to be complete different opinions! (You did read the previous chapters?)

My questions are:

1) What can we safely assume to be a healthy ideal relationship?

2) I'd also like to know to what degree are our biological instincts similar, and why do we differ.

3) What does our creator really expect from us, how do we know when our leaders, teachers, preachers and medical experts are divinely inspired regarding this topic?

4) If the concubine concept is correct, what about the other "less successful males? What is the ratio of woman to men, does it provide for a concubine concept?

5) Would the concubine theory provide a stronger gene pool for the human race much the same way a dominant male of the animal kingdom provides the strongest off spring for the herd? (Yeah, are we really just animals?)

Time line comments:
Well it's been 7months and I'm still experiencing a response from my "rabbit attachment" when it is exposed to my wife when she gets out the shower. Even when I'm miffed with her, the lower half forgives within a blink of her thigh! So I do feel it is some or other sensor that has been designed to let my human program know that it has targeted the purpose of human existence.

Once more this confirms the probability of my machine theory, let's assume we're all programs of some sort, and the male attachment is merely the males sensor running subconsciously to enlighten its host to mating opportunities, thus ensuring the human existence for another generation!

Make sense? You decide for yourself.

Chapter 26: The Power Of Humility

When one of the two partners feel they have experienced or learnt a powerful new truth, (or God forbid, the ultimate truth) there are certain beyond imagination conflicts simply waiting for the enlightened partner to place his/her foot right in the middle of a huge pile of emotional poo!

Now we can argue for hours as to which sex is the most guilty of this crime, with no real success. The secret is avoiding all and any forms of dictation.

Imagine this scenario, "Hey. Sweetie, I have the answer to life, the universe and all its problems, **YOU** fail to see what **I'VE** just discovered, I'm right, and, well, you're not!" Is this more than likely going to chase away any life signs of an active nymph gland?

I'm sure this story would have had quite a different ending should the characters listened and been a bit more humble?

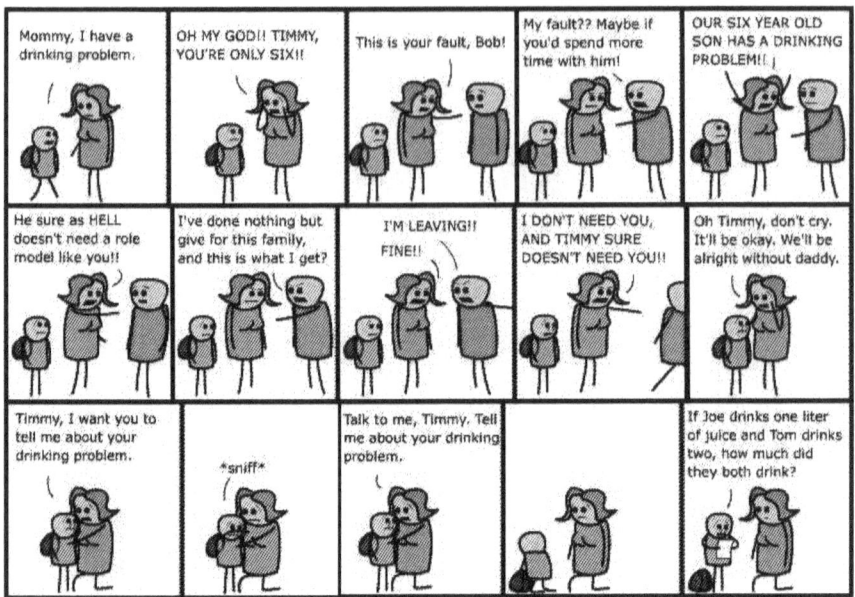

Face it humanoid of any sex, whether confused, or "normal/straight", no one really likes a smart ass. Yes, just like us straight, chemically balanced, or hormonally correct, testarone well adjusted people; the gays and lesbians also have problems with relationships. And despite the success stories that can be written about bullies, no one likes them either, we simply let them get their way. So if you have just discovered the solution to relationships, be really careful how you share this with your partner, it might just cost you yours!

Now how many times have you seen some one playing guitar, and thought to yourself, "I'd like to do that." Or at the beach commented, "That looks like fun" when watching some one surfing. In these and similar occasions we're attracted to someone doing something they get enjoyment from. Imagine you're sitting at home on a rainy day and your spouse suggests that you must now learn to surf – your reply received just might be "Are you fucking insane?"

The lesson is to motivate and lead the way, not dictate. Human nature is such that we enjoy creative situations on average, and most people like to have fun. So when we see the joy that can be attained from a certain pass time we consider trying to take part in it. Our enthusiasm and passion for this new pass time can often result in us expecting our partner to join us!

What I'm trying to say folks is lead by example, don't push some one, rather expose a fun concept to someone than tell them that they must experience this new fun. There a much more reasonable chance they might want to join you.

This can be said for "truths" too. An opinion or life style can lead to content or contempt. If the life style or truth you have discovered is wonderful, live it, see what fruits it bears. If the rewards are great you stand a much better chance of not just your partner becoming interested in it, but also friends, children and family.

Learn from the error of the old school churches who hold the fear of fire and hell if you don't follow the leaders and representatives of God. Don't lay guilt on some one, or fear of great loss if they choose another direction or alternative.

Humility is powerful, this is the decision to live and show, not to become adamant and arrogant. (Hey, notice how words in certain contexts, whether opposite or similar, often sound almost the same?)

I can understand the frustration that often accompanies humility when we view bombastic people who enforce their thought, this normally does rectify itself, but might take a lifetime or more before it happens, which is not really cool for the humble who might be dead before the change takes place.

Another quote from one of my favorite musicians, Frank Zappa, was on the lines of "The meek will inherit the earth, if there's anything left after the bullies have pillaged it."

So we have to draw a fine line between humility and letting ourselves be trod on. We must somehow learn the cross over between leading by example and saying "Listen, dickweed, stop being so bluddy stupid, can't you see I'm right!" So I think the secret to success is as follows:

1) Never confront some one in public, especially if you're convinced you're right. If you prove to be, there's a damn good chance the now rectified person might hate you for embarrassing them and pointing out their ignorance in public.

2) Think carefully before you speak, incorrectly phrased comments can mislead someone as to your true intentions. Start of with a comment like "You must be stupid to think that….." And you're criticizing the person and making them feel bad for making a mistake. They become defensive and you've almost lost before you've begun. A mistake by definition is not intentional; very few people choose to take advantage of people, those that do often end up in some or other parliament.

3) Listen to the persons point when they share why they think the way they do; this makes one feel that their thoughts have value. Ever considered that they might know some thing that you don't? This small fact might even result in you changing your own opinion! Who knows, perhaps after listening to them you can help them see a possible error in their thought, hence turning the situation around. The result being a shared and respected conversation with a positive outcome.

4) Don't be too proud, if you're wrong, admit it, and allow yourself to be helped, this in turn is almost a guarantee that future discussions will be met with a sincere mind to get to the best solution.

5) Find the right time to chat with the person you wish to share your opinions with, timing is vital! Imagine your spouse demands your attention while you're trying to work on something, or just before you go to sleep and your eyes are flapping into distance sleepy oblivion.

Now back to our book topic, the nymph glands transition into hibernation.

Imagine your partner has just embarrassed you in front of your peers at a party. They have successfully pointed out why your understanding of a certain social skill, like scratching your butt in public is best avoided, and if you must, then try and be discreet about it. (Hey ask your partner to scratch your butt for you – just kidding) So you are now made aware that your efforts to appease this need have not been successfully done outside public eye.

Well even if your spouse was not right about you as you have been successfully hiding this deed, all your friends will make a note of trying to catch you doing some anal excavations.

You're now rather peeved, angry, embarrassed. Later your spouse wants to make love to you, to share that same, now unscratched butt, in a sweaty pleasurable exchange of body fluids. The chances of success? – not really much! Who wants to share this level of intimacy with the one who just made you the village idiot?

Once more discretion is the call of the day. If you have a problem with some ones habits, talk to them. All I'm suggesting is the following:

1) Do it one on one.

2) Pick the right time to discuss the issue with them.

3) NEVER condescend to them.

4) If it's urgent, ask them, with a sincere smile if you may please speak in private with them.

Humility, tact and concern for your partners' emotional and social standing will greatly increase the chances of the nun gland not being stimulated.

I guess we can call this approach "respect"?

Chapter 27: Children, The Result Of The Nymph Gland

So why did I leave this chapter for last? Simple! When setting out to do something we need to have a goal, or completion of sorts. In a way a child is the goal of completion of the nymph gland and willy function. Without the child the human species cannot go on, and I believe a good start is essential. We all started as children.

My other wish in this book is that our children have the most wonderful childhood, after all, please forgive this cliché, they are the adults of tomorrow, just like you and I were a few decades ago. Is the below cartoon one of the scenario's you might have answered when avoiding embarrassing questions?

Yeah, I also had the stork fed to me, this along with Father X-mas, the Easter Bunny, The Tooth Fairy, Monsters in the closet, and all the stereo type nonsense our children catch us out with eventually. So how do we expect them to respect us when we tell them about AIDS, pregnancy, STD's?

If my theory is correct about programming, then it explains their reluctance to believe other 'stories' we feed them when they're bigger. The idea is really simple, as young receivers of facts from their folks they're exposed to "little white lies" which are real important to you when you're 3 to 6 years old. So when you find that certain really fussed about truths are bogus your new programming asks you to question other facts provided to you. Interesting don't you think?

With this in mind it's no wonder we grow up to be doubting adults. The most important things in our lives were shattered as kids, or at the least we learnt the art of mistrusting myths, and even questioning other adults. Faith is sooo important for any person, no-matter your age.

Now my next claim is that some of us grew up to realize that these lies (Father X-mas, Tooth Fairy, etc..) were not intentional, but for excuses to 'give' us things, yep in a weird round about way it's an expected fashion to lie to our kids to give them hope, some thing to look forward to.

Then a few years later we end the scam or we're caught out! The worst part for me is that society frowns upon those who wish **not** to mislead and fabricate Tooth Fairies. (Or was it actually the tooth mouse?) You did hear the phrase "Bah, humbug?" Go watch Scrooge sometime.

Now for me kids are the most honest, sincere trusting humans to live among us. So why do so many homosapiens end up being skeptical, hesitant, lie, doubtful? You've just read the first few paragraphs of this chapter and you still don't know? Duh?

Let us return to the nymph gland topic. Well I have two wonderful children, one that has been lost for some time and I can only hope I'll have a chance to meet her again, perhaps as an adult. The worst part for me is the years I can never get back. Similarly for her she has lost her father due to her mother using her a tool to hurt me. Jeez, now I'm sidetracked again, sorry.

The other is my stunning son, all 5yrs of toddling around my life – he's awesome! I feel so lousy scamming him with the NORM regarding all the society approved lies. I just hope he understands that I didn't want him to think he's dad was lying at the age 3 to 8 (or whenever he realizes there no fat dude with a red costume and white beard giving him gifts after watching his behavior for the past year – yes folks, many a parent has said 'behave now or Father X-mas isn't going to bring you toys'.) Is this the only hold we have over our child's discipline? So in turn I hope he forgives me after catching me out at 8(when ever).

If only we gave our children the truth from day one they might just have a higher percentage turnout of honest adults? An interesting concept that I doubt will ever be tried and tested. Sort of sad?

We need to bear in mind that every adult, without exception, began as a child. Sort of the same way a divorce needs a marriage? Now there's a biblical scripture that says the following: "The sins of the father get passed on to the children". This for me backs up my argument that we as adults need to break our misconceptions learnt as children. We can do this by not passing on bogus stories, in other words passing the sins from the father to the child, this in turn gives the children an advantage when starting life.

In other words they need not have to deal with the 3 to 5 years of awareness of nonsense, like Father Xmas – yep, he's a huge Christian representative folks – all in the name of Christ's birthday that we are NOT commanded to celebrate! What a let down! Please bear in mind that at the age of 8 or so, for a child to learn his folks are bogus, this shatters over 70% of his life existence's experience, no wonder we grow up so screwed!

They say that the eyes are the windows to the soul. With this in mind, please take the time to notice the look in your child's eyes. Their innocence and eagerness to accept our 'truths' is amazing. Then look at many adults and see how they question you when you look into their eyes! I really hope you can see this, it's a revelation!

Never forget that this is how we began our exploration of life, as a child! It's up to us to choose if we want the wheel to keep turning, or to give our children something to believe in!

I was also initially going to write a few paragraphs about more physical abuse on children, those who suffered rape. They often avoid a healthy sex life as it reminds them of their worse nightmares! I've decided against it as it makes me want to explode. May those that are guilty be reported.

But for those that are or were victims, you must tell some one, report that evil sick shit for what they are. By not doing so you're allowing a pedophile to continue their perverted spree, this in turn means you're almost an accomplice as you have the power but did nothing!

There's more ways to kill a nymph gland than today's stresses. The experiences from yesterday come back to haunt many at the most inconvenient time! Not that reporting will cure a nymph gland, but it sure as hell can thwart many others dying the same way. Learn from your experience and do your best to prevent other from the same suffering.

Time line comments:
Oh yeah, this is a classic story that just happened a few minutes ago. I had just finished giving a lesson and asked my student what exam he was about to write. He replied it was a subject called 'life orientation', and he was to write about the disease called AIDS, for the 7th time he said with a hint of contempt for the topic.

It's so ironic that our ex 2nd in charge of South Africa, Jacob Zuma, didn't even know about how AIDS can be contracted, how did this slip by a person of his stature and responsibility. What impression does a man like this leave on out children's minds? With this style of leadership being tolerated is it any wonder why SA is experiencing high fatalities as a result of this disease?

So here we have a kid who's really had enough of having the AIDS awareness being forced down his throat. He knows what a condom is, while some politicians think that a shower cures AIDS! Are we not focusing our awareness in the wrong direction?

He left laughing after I shared my opinion with him. It's amazing how these and other world leaders side step their own shortcomings while pointing out other nations and people faults, possibly hoping to distract from their own sins? Just a thought.

Treat your child how you would like to have been treated when you were young. Adults do have the power to ensure a better quality of generation for the future.

The joy from making a child happy is wonderful!

Chapter 28: My Personal Rules / Advice

This list is some guidelines that have helped me the cope or focus while existing on this blue planet. They are not listed in order of priority. Please realize that I often question my own values and beliefs as the truth is so elusive on occasion that my human program has difficulty keeping up with the philosophies that I try and formulate to guide my decisions.

1) Try your best to love the one you chose, even if they do change, if they say they still love you, believe them. Perhaps they've got stresses on work or personal levels that might cause you to doubt them. Often we hide our worries from our partner on the ground that we don't want them to worry too. Even though this never works out, as we normally know when our spouse is worried, their heart is in the right place.

2) Listen to your partner's beliefs or views – they are often right. And if not, at least you can understand why they act the way the do. There are very few people that are naturally evil and nasty. Most of us really want to be happy and share this with others. It's how we make ourselves happy that causes problems.

3) Don't place the responsibility of your happiness on your spouse. Make yourself happy first, get a hobby, lead your partner, and not blame them for lack of satisfaction. I cannot begin to describe the amount of satisfaction I got while writing this book.

4) Don't let sex, or rather lack of sex get you down. Try masturbating, once "relieved" all the desires die down. Our drive, especially from men, is largely chemical interaction screwing with our mind. (Excuse the intentional pun) If lack of sex is a problem, masturbate – it only takes a few minutes, and then the hormonal drive subsides and then let your hobby keep you busy. Too

many uncontrolled hormonal imbalances have cost children their family, not to mention the risk of STD's. I'd rather screw my hand than some ones emotions.

5) Make yourself happy. Yes I know I'm repeating point 3, but I believe that too many people don't realize this. Show those around you it's possible, be creative! If people see you're happy and not relying on your spouse for happiness they're bound to follow. We live in a time of wonderful opportunities – use them dammit!!

6) With the odds of anyone actually claiming to have the absolute truth be extremely cautious. This is equally valid for trusting a political party. It's only really the leaders that benefit from their decisions.

Well this my shortest chapter, I guess the bible hits this one on the head when it says, "Do unto others as you'd have them do unto you". But one last thought provoker before we wrap up the book. Have you noticed that for almost every saying there's an opposite saying with the same strength of logic? Here's a quick example "Many hands make light work – Too many cooks spoil the broth."

Aren't we the clever ones? We have conveniently made an escape for almost any situation we find ourselves in! Let your choices and conscience guide you. As Mr. Spock would say, "Go forth and prosper".

Conclusion

Well, after reading my personal experience I'd like to sum up my feelings, beliefs, attitudes, etc.

On marriage:
I'm not entirely convinced that the western "Christian" approach to marriage is ideal. Remember life B.C.? – see the concubine theory. There are far too many divorces to reinforce that something in the "one man, one woman" plot is not right.

Despite this I do think that some couples can co exist in a healthy social and sexual relationship. I do think that too many couples subscribe to the theory of "better the devil you know than the devil you don't know!" In other words too many people try and force two wonderful people to live together that really are not that compatible.

Perhaps we fear failure so much we refuse to admit that our choice might have been wrong, so we get engaged, marry and live a life of trying to adapt to our partner.

Men and woman's needs:
I heard a saying that men hope their spouse doesn't change – and then she does! Similarly woman hope their husband changes and they don't." This is destined to failure, as both grow further apart.

If we marry with the hope our partner will make us happy we're in it for the wrong reason. I think we should rather find contentment in our careers, our hobbies and the knowledge that someone loves us. This way our expectations lie in something, not someone. It's easier and a lot less heartbreaking swapping a "something."

It's not going to hurt our child if we exchange one career for a better one that makes us feel more successful and benefits the family. Imagine the responsibility of relying on our spouse for happiness while they're relying on you – it's a no win situation when we blame our partner for failure or lack of understanding. (Even unintentionally)

Religion:
This is a tough one for me. At the time of typing this I'm not sure how to categorize myself. I know I'm not a Christian although I do believe there must be a creator and I do think the basic Bible concepts and morals are wonderful. (It's the people running the churches I doubt)

I do agree with the bible's attitude of "Search for the truth and you will find it." What the bible doesn't really tell me is when I can safely assume that I have the truth! (See the chapter on religions.) If you think about it, if we assume we have found the truth then we can safely assume we no longer need to look for it.

This in turn cancels out our search, which means we no longer have to heed this message. I think we might only receive the truth at death, assuming we're not going to end up as worm food. I also often wonder if man has created religion because he cannot deal with lack of immortality. Hey, we'd all like to live forever?

Sex:
Doctors and experts tell us that only the human and dolphins enjoy this exchange of body fluids. Wow, it's comforting to know that someone with years of study and a university degree confirms my basic instincts regarding a good screw!

The problem I have is that perhaps boys and girls want it for very different reasons due to our body's design, or rather our hormonal driven mechanics. I think that many woman use sex to get a partner for procreation and security. While the male species really enjoys sex and sometimes treat their partners as a commodity, or rather an accessory. (No, I do not condone or agree with that notion.) Let's look at why I think this might be true:

1) The woman's sex drive often decreases after birth. Single and divorced women are possibly often more open to casual sex to "lure" in a partner while a married woman believes she has snared her mate and the occasional "duty" to her husband is enough. To validate this have you ever seen the stats on woman faking orgasms? Go ask your doctor!

2) The male sex drive is not altered by marriage. All the men I have spoken with confirm this; we still enjoy sex no matter what stage of our life we're in or the family status. This is why I think many men have affairs while married, I don't think it's the outside relationship that's important, it the sexual satisfaction that the male hormone demands from the brain. If this was not so shouldn't there be an equal amount of men and women prostitutes?

The human race:
I've learnt so much about myself while writing this book that I'd strongly encourage both men and women to write their own findings down, even if not for publication, just to learn and help understand ourselves and those we love.

After considering my theory that perhaps the human is not really so special, I'm more prepared to except that I'm an intricate machine with an awareness that can be encouraged to alter it's values with drug or alcohol use, or abuse.

Personally I'm quite okay with accepting I'm software that Bill Gates wishes he wrote. Or maybe not – the human race is too inconsistent and has far to many faults; we're definitely not the most stable of programs are we?

The facts below often make me embarrassed to be part of the human race:

1) Mankind has caused extinction of many animals and fish.

2) Mankind has damaged the Ozone

3) Mankind has created pollution.

4) Mankind kills it's own species in the name of religion and greed by the millions.

5) We refuse to share our wealth with the needy, although those in charge try and make the average take responsibility.

6) The majority often follows a minority (governments) even when we believe them to be wrong. We give way to bullies!

Face it – are we our own worst enemy?

Are we machines?

Although I'd love to think of myself as a spirit I find too many facts to suggest other wise, here are a few examples.

1) Compare sex to a pressure cooker, when the steam build up is high, make the valve open, the steam is released and the cooking continues happily, don't do this and "bang"! With sex, the male hormone goes ballistic, release your valve (Your "willy") and you'll be surprised how your drive subsides. So you have to control the valve by hand – it's better than going "bang" with someone.

2) Stimulants such as drugs and alcohol can alter and change your morals and standards. Throw some sugar in your cars petrol and the car won't work, it's not the cars fault! Similarly be careful what you throw inside yourself. It's your choice and the after effect can break your ride too.

3) Ride your vehicle too hard, too fast and too far and you run out of petrol or it breaks. The human body uses sleep as part of it's petrol; this combined with food gives us what we deem a healthy and sound body and mind. If we were not a machine this would not occur. Similarly the brain, the housing for our "free will" follows the same approach, our thoughts can get seriously altered if simply tired. Next time you see some one over tired, notice how irritable or irrational they are.

So how do I think we should live?

Wow, I'm not too sure, but here's a short list, not in order of priority.

1) Search for the truth.

2) Don't believe everything you hear – you have a brain!

3) Don't screw with someone's emotions – it hurts!

4) Exercise concern for those around you.

5) Love and educate your children.

6) If you know better, share! (But exercise tact when doing so.)

7) Love your partner.

8) Take responsibility.

9) There are certain mechanical requirements for your body – fulfill them!

10) If you don't understand ask. The only dumb question is the silent one!

11) Be creative – think!

12) Charity begins at home – make yourself happy first.

13) Don't expect satisfaction from your partner, this is a bonus, not a right!

14) Lead by example – don't dictate.

15) Don't accept everything the TV tells you.

16) Don't believe everything a religious or political leader tells you.

17) Choose your life partner very, very carefully.

18) If responding to animal instinct and need sex, wear a condom!

19) Listen – it's the only way to learn.

20) Make children one of your priorities, they're the next in line to take over your accomplishments.

In short: "Do unto others as you have them do unto you" – the Bible.

ABOUT THE AUTHOR

I am 41 year old musician and guitar teacher who is enjoying a wonderful second marriage. To learn about the first marriage please read the book.

I live for my children, an extremely close second place is my wife, and then my dog.

In the non-living world I love music, nothing beats the thrill of performing and watching people having fun while the band entertains them. So my favourites here are my guitars, and then my motorbike.

I'm fascinated about humans, how we work, and our spiritual connection to who-ever our creator might be. (I do believe in a creator, or creators.) I really hope and wish more of us would realise why and who infuence our decisions and take better control of this.

I love sharing theories and try to validate them - this is why I wrote the book. I do not believe I have all the answers, or the complete truth. But I wish to learn.

I believe charity begins at home, so how can I make those around me happy if I'm not happy myself? And this happiness can be better attained if I understand what influences my everyday life...